Planet Earth

FLOOD

This volume is one of a series that examines the workings of the planet earth, from the geological wonders of its continents to the marvels of its atmosphere and its ocean depths.

Cover
The seething torrent of the Arno River rips away embankments and surges through the ancient streets of Florence, Italy, during the great flood of 1966. The cataclysm submerged parts of the city beneath 20 feet of muddy water, destroying some of the greatest artworks known to the Western world and leaving a stinking, polluted quagmire in its wake.

Planet Earth

FLOOD

By Champ Clark
and The Editors of Time-Life Books

Time-Life Books, Alexandria, Virginia

Time-Life Books Inc.
is a wholly owned subsidiary of

TIME INCORPORATED

FOUNDER: Henry R. Luce 1898-1967

Editor-in-Chief: Henry Anatole Grunwald
President: J. Richard Munro
Chairman of the Board: Ralph P. Davidson
Executive Vice President: Clifford J. Grum
Chairman, Executive Committee: James R. Shepley
Editorial Director: Ralph Graves
Group Vice President, Books: Joan D. Manley
Vice Chairman: Arthur Temple

TIME-LIFE BOOKS INC.

MANAGING EDITOR: Jerry Korn
Text Director: George Constable
Board of Editors: Dale M. Brown, George G. Daniels,
Thomas H. Flaherty Jr., Martin Mann, Philip W. Payne,
Gerry Schremp, Gerald Simons, Kit van Tulleken
Planning Director: Edward Brash
Art Director: Tom Suzuki
  Assistant: Arnold C. Holeywell
Director of Administration: David L. Harrison
Director of Operations: Gennaro C. Esposito
Director of Research: Carolyn L. Sackett
  Assistant: Phyllis K. Wise
Director of Photography: Dolores A. Littles

CHAIRMAN: John D. McSweeney
President: Carl G. Jaeger
Executive Vice Presidents: John Steven Maxwell,
David J. Walsh
Vice Presidents: George Artandi, Stephen L. Bair,
Peter G. Barnes, Nicholas Benton, John L. Canova,
Beatrice T. Dobie, Carol Flaumenhaft, James L. Mercer,
Herbert Sorkin, Paul R. Stewart

PLANET EARTH

EDITOR: George G. Daniels
Senior Editor: Thomas A. Lewis
Designer: Donald Komai
Chief Researcher: Pat S. Good

Editorial Staff for *Flood*
Picture Editor: Carol Forsyth Mickey
Writers: William C. Banks, Jan Leslie Cook, Gus Hedberg,
Roger Herst, John Newton, David Thiemann
Researchers: Blaine Reilly Marshall and
Oliver G. A. M. Payne
Assistant Designer: Susan K. White
Copy Coordinator: Victoria Lee
Picture Coordinator: Donna Quaresima
Editorial Assistant: Annette T. Wilkerson

Editorial Operations
Production Director: Feliciano Madrid
  Assistants: Peter A. Inchauteguiz, Karen A. Meyerson
Copy Processing: Gordon E. Buck
Quality Control Director: Robert L. Young
  Assistant: James J. Cox
  Associates: Daniel J. McSweeney, Michael G. Wight
Art Coordinator: Anne B. Landry
Copy Room Director: Susan B. Galloway
  Assistants: Celia Beattie, Ricki Tarlow

Correspondents: Elisabeth Kraemer (Bonn); Margot
Hapgood, Dorothy Bacon (London); Susan Jonas, Lucy T.
Voulgaris (New York); Maria Vincenza Aloisi, Josephine
du Brusle (Paris); Ann Natanson (Rome). Valuable
assistance was also provided by: Helga Kohl (Bonn);
Dwight V. Gast (Florence); Enid Farmer (Lexington,
Massachusetts); Karin B. Pearce, Millicent Trowbridge
(London); Trini Bandres (Madrid); Miriam Hsia (New
York); M. T. Hirschkoff (Paris); Ed Reingold, Eiko
Fukuda, Masoo Murata, Katsuko Yamazaki (Tokyo).

For information about any Time-Life book, please write:
Reader Information
Time-Life Books
541 North Fairbanks Court
Chicago, Illinois 60611

Library of Congress Cataloguing in Publication Data
Clark, Champ.
Flood.
    (Planet earth; 3)
    Bibliography p.
    Includes index.
    1. Floods.   I. Time-Life Books.   II. Title.
III. Series.
GB1399.C55   551.48'9   81-18545
ISBN 0-8094-4308-2   AACR2
ISBN 0-8094-4309-0 (lib. bdg.)
ISBN 0-8094-4310-4 (mail order ed.)

THE AUTHOR

Champ Clark, a veteran of 23 years as a correspondent, writer and senior editor for *Time,* retired from weekly journalism in 1972 in order to freelance and teach in the English Department at the University of Virginia. He is the author of *The Badlands* in the Time-Life Books series The American Wilderness. As a resident of Kansas City he observed firsthand the workings of the Weather Service and became interested in the subject matter of this volume.

THE CONSULTANTS

M. Gordon Wolman is Chairman of the Department of Geography and Environmental Engineering at The Johns Hopkins University. A Fellow of the American Academy of Arts and Sciences, Dr. Wolman has traveled throughout the world studying and lecturing on a variety of environmental and flood- and river-related problems. He is the author of more than 50 articles and papers in these fields.

Sidney Horenstein is a geologist in the Department of Invertebrates at the American Museum of Natural History and a faculty member of the Department of Geology at City University of New York. He organized and served as coordinator of the Environmental Information Center of the American Museum.

CONTENTS

FLORENCE'S ORDEAL BY FLOOD

It is the simplest substance on earth, merely two atoms of hydrogen and one of oxygen. Early philosophers embraced it as the fundamental building block of the universe, the wellspring of life itself—and they were not far wrong. It bathes the world with countless forms: a spring spurting from a mountainside, the glassy mirror of a still lake, a river gliding silently to the sea.

But water—this beneficent liquid, so tranquil, soft and tractable—has a murderous Janus face as well. Once loosed from channels and basins, water races overland powered by gravity. At flood stage, the smallest stream is a thundering torrent; water less than knee-deep can knock a man down and drown him. Houses are flimsy arks: Huge waves, 1,000-ton walls of water, can tear buildings from their foundations and send them careening downstream.

Such catastrophes have overwhelmed men since Noah's time; there have been thousands of them. One of the best documented is the 1966 inundation of Florence, cradle of the Italian Renaissance. On the night of November 3, the city was lulled to sleep by a hard, steady rain; the next morning it woke to a low, terrifying rumble and found the Arno River raging through the streets.

Statistics tell of some losses: 35 dead, 5,000 homeless, 15,000 cars destroyed. The damage to books, paintings, frescoes and sculpture cannot be reckoned. But the true horror is preserved only in searing images of a city vanishing beneath the flood.

"A tumultuous mass of water stretches from bank to bank; its surface twisting with ropes of water that smack together in spouts of foam," wrote Kathrine Kressmann Taylor, an American eyewitness. "Down the first street back from the river, water is pent wall to wall within the canyon of the buildings. It plunges into the square in a vortex of waves, whirlpools and debris—branches, twigs, shoes, pocketbooks and paper, which swing round in a crazy bobbing dance."

In such a cataclysm, conventional descriptions may be infuriatingly inadequate. "At ten o'clock," Kathrine Taylor wrote, "there is another news broadcast: 'Florence is a lake,' they report, an absurdly placid metaphor, this!"

Beneath a rain-filled sky, the roiling Arno River overtops bridges and embankments and surges through the ancient streets of Florence. In the 1966 flood virtually every Renaissance landmark was damaged, including the famed Palazzo Vecchio (*center*), onetime home of a Medici prince.

Where a two-lane riverfront avenue once ran, receding waters reveal broken pavement, a yawning chasm and the naked foundations of nearby buildings. The Arno floodwaters carried away one million cubic yards of land and rubble.

After scribing a black high-water ring 12 feet above the sidewalk, a pond of fuel oil lingers in a piazza two blocks from the river. Oil gushed from thousands of basement tanks during the flood, contaminating everything it touched and posing a severe fire hazard.

A mound of muddy refuse—smashed chairs, sodden
office files, books—lies on a battered bridge across
the Arno after being bulldozed from nearby streets.
Heavy equipment from all over Italy worked
for four weeks to clear the city of muck and debris.

The Ponte Vecchio, home to jewelers and goldsmiths since the 16th Century, stands battered after the flood. Though the Arno literally rushed through this famous landmark, the artisans rebuilt their gutted shops and were back in business within a few months.

Chapter 1

IN ALL LANDS WHERE WATER FLOWS

The flood continued forty days upon the earth; and the waters increased, and bore up the ark, and it rose high above the earth. . . . And the waters prevailed so mightily upon the earth that all the high mountains under the whole heaven were covered."

The Old Testament account of Noah and the Deluge, that enduring saga of Biblical man's great adventure in a time of natural cataclysm, is but one among many down through the ages. Since the dawn of civilization, human cultures in nearly all lands have clung to legends of monstrous floods that were believed to have ravaged the entire face of the earth.

The Scriptural story itself was in all likelihood borrowed by the Hebrew narrators of Genesis from the ancient Babylonians, who attributed the global flood of their folk memory to an insomniac god named Enlil. This deity, it seems, was enraged because humans were making too much noise. "The uproar of mankind is intolerable," he cried, "and sleep is no longer possible by reason of the babble." After several unsuccessful efforts to shush humanity by the sending of deadly plagues, Enlil finally caused the worst of all the catastrophes at his command—a flood.

One Norse myth offers a worldwide flood brought about by the gushing blood of an evil god who had been slain by Odin and his two brothers. Aristotle, that supremely sophisticated Greek, accepted as fact the story of how Prometheus saved the human race from extinction by warning his son Deucalion of a calamitous global flood. And Lithuanian lore tells of a god named Pramzinas who created the great flood and then sat eating nuts while peering down to inspect the damage; he dropped one of the celestial nutshells onto a mountaintop, thus providing a handy vessel in which a few survivors gratefully floated until the ruinous waters receded.

Flood legends are especially abundant among the Indians of North and South America. Chippewa tribesmen of Minnesota and North Dakota, where long, bitter winters are often followed by damaging spring thaws, solemnly recounted how a little mouse gnawed a hole through the skin of a leather bag in which the sun's heat was trapped; this melted all the ice and snow in the world, causing a gigantic flood. According to Mexico's Quiche Indians, the gods made mankind of clay but botched the job (for one thing, people could not turn their heads); a flood was sent to wipe out the defective race so that the creators could start all over again.

Such legends doubtless had their remote origins in very real floods of vast dimensions and destructive power. Some years ago, British archeologists digging near the dead city of Ur, on the Euphrates River in what is now Iraq,

Massive sheets of floodwater from the Nishnabotna River, a tributary of the Missouri, surge across the Iowa prairie toward the town of Hamburg in this classic aerial photo of a river on the rampage. The 1952 flood inundated more than 66,000 acres of farmland, but the people who were in its path had been forewarned and escaped to safety.

In a 15th Century French manuscript painting inspired by the Biblical account of the Deluge, Noah, his family and a menagerie of birds and beasts emerge from the Ark as the floodwaters recede.

came upon a layer of clay eight feet thick that clearly had been deposited by water *(page 21)*. That flood may in fact have been the Biblical Deluge; as the leader of the British expedition noted, "For the people who lived there, that was all the world."

To frail mortals struggling for survival amid the distended and devouring waters of a great flood, it may indeed appear that the entire earth has been stricken. Yet for various meteorological and geological reasons, a single catastrophic flood of global proportions is impossible.

Modern man's Biblical forefathers had at least an inkling of a phenomenon that has since come to be known as the hydrologic cycle. "All the rivers run into the sea," said Ecclesiastes 1:7, "yet the sea is never full; unto the place from whence the rivers come thither they return again."

For perhaps three billion years the total amount of water on the earth and in its atmosphere has been almost exactly the same. With the help of the sun's heat and the pull of gravity, it is forever recycled, now evaporating and entering the air as vapor, then condensing and falling back to earth as rain or snow. Thus the water in which this morning's eggs were boiled may be the same as that once drawn from the Nile for Cleopatra's bath.

The hydrologic cycle imposes certain limitations affecting the size of floods. If all the water in the atmosphere at any given time were suddenly to be loosed upon the earth, it would cover the planet to a depth of only a fraction of an inch; any deluge that inundated the highlands of the Ararat-Caucasus-Elburz region, where Noah's Ark reputedly came at last to ground, must have covered the earth to thousands of feet above mean sea level.

The profusion of legends thus testifies not to a single flood that engulfed the entire planet but to the awesome multiplicity of floods that have afflicted man, wherever he dwelt, since his first days upon the earth. Floods strike in myriad forms, including sea surges driven by wild winds or tsunamis churned into fury by seismic activity. But by far the most frequent, standing in a class by themselves, are the inland, fresh-water floods that are caused by rain, by the melting of snow and ice or, with cruel irony, by the bursting of the very bulwarks that man has erected to protect himself and his belongings from angry waters.

From majestic rivers to country creeks, from mountain rills to the tiny trickles that occasionally damp otherwise arid wastelands, every stream on earth is subject to flooding, at some time, under certain conditions. Of all natural hazards, floods are the most far-flung—and the most ruinous to life and property. One study of natural disasters found that between the years 1947 and 1967, no fewer than 173,170 persons had died as a direct result of riverine floods—as opposed to a grand total of 269,635 dead in 18 other categories of catastrophe, including hurricanes, tornadoes, earthquakes and volcanoes.

Death by drowning, the specter of helpless humans being swallowed by choking waters, is of course the aspect most grimly associated with floods. Yet floods take their terrible toll in countless other ways. Staggering numbers of persons may be left without shelter; in 1955, floods throughout northern India devastated hundreds of villages, leaving tens of thousands homeless. And famine may stalk the land after the livestock and crops upon which nations depend for their sustenance are obliterated.

Paradoxically, major floods are often accompanied by fire as power lines are broken and gas mains are ruptured. Communications and transportation systems are disrupted as telephone lines go down, bridges are washed out, highways and railroad tracks are torn asunder.

All too obviously, floods cannot distinguish among living creatures—a fact that sometimes leads to results that are particularly horrifying to man. In India and Pakistan, people seeking refuge in treetops have died in agony from the bites of venomous snakes. In some floods, rats are driven from their normal habitats to spread disease and even to contest with humans for scanty food supplies. The floodwaters themselves are often contaminating, and such epizootic diseases as cholera and typhoid can make their deadly mark in the wake of major floods.

Despite their clear potential for peril, flood plains have always held an irresistible attraction for people. In the plain of the Tigris and Euphrates Rivers of Mesopotamia, one of the earliest agricultural civilizations flourished on rich alluvial soils that had been washed down by the flooding rivers. (According to one estimate, as many as one and a half billion people—one third of the world's population—still depend upon alluvial soils for their food.) Subsequent civilizations have capitalized on other advantages of flood plains. Rivers themselves are arteries for commerce and communications, and towns and cities have burgeoned on or near the banks of rivers everywhere; in the United

States alone, nearly 3,800 settlements each containing 2,500 people or more are prone to flooding.

Just as man has responded to the enticements of flood plains, he has tirelessly and ingeniously devised methods of fending off threatening waters. He has built dams to divert or regulate floods, diversion channels to share the burden of a flood with the main river, and levees or embankments to contain rising waters. In places where such sophisticated measures are impossible, man copes with floods in other ways. Thus the tribesmen of Barotseland in northwest Zambia have a conditioned and highly realistic response: When the annual rains arrive, they simply pick up and move to high ground to wait out the Zambezi River floods.

Such migrations are unthinkable for urban dwellers; for them the only recourse is to forecast impending floods and issue timely warnings. For more than a century on many large rivers, the arrivals of their flood crests at particular points have been accurately predicted almost as if they were running on railroad timetables. By contrast, forecasting flash floods, which generally afflict smaller streams, is a young and inexact science. Today's meteorologists and hydrologists are armed with the most sophisticated technology—radar equipment, satellites, computers, and automatic stream-level and precipitation sensors— but the weather is still so unpredictable, the elements contributing to floods so numerous and the areas at risk so widespread that a forecast often comes down to cool individual judgment.

As sudden and as savage as flash floods caused by precipitation may be, they pale in comparison with the spectacular eruptions of water that are let loose by the bursting of man-made dams. Almost from the beginning of man's endless efforts to control his environment, he has built barriers to contain rivers. Today, throughout the world, dams stand as massive monuments to human engineering; it was estimated in 1978 that the reservoirs created by dams regulate more than 20 per cent of all the water that runs off the earth in North America and Africa, 15 per cent in Europe and 14 per cent in Asia.

But dams are subjected to pressures beyond imagining. Their reservoirs impound colossal amounts of water. Lake Mead behind Hoover Dam on the Colorado River is 115 miles long and has a capacity of 1.4 trillion cubic feet of water, or a fantastic 10.5 trillion gallons. The volume of water impounded behind dams is so enormous, in fact, that hydrologists have devised a more manageable measure called acre-feet. One acre-foot is the equivalent of one acre of land covered by water to a depth of one foot. In the case of Lake Mead, the figure comes to 32 million.

Water itself is extremely heavy. A gallon weighs about 8.5 pounds, a cubic foot weighs about 62 pounds and a large bathful (one cubic yard) weighs about three quarters of a ton. And while a well-designed, properly located and soundly constructed dam may remain safe for hundreds of years, the dam has never been built that could forever withstand wear and exposure and the hydrostatic pressures that build up within its reservoir. Dams must be regularly inspected and repaired; if not, the tiniest flaw can become an engulfing disaster.

Because of the calamities they cause, floods are indelibly engraved on human consciousness as agents of death and destruction. But floods have the duality of Janus; just as they present the face of ruin, so too they can bring measureless bounties and blessings. It was hardly coincidental that the ancient Egyptians called their country Black Land, in honor of the rich mud carried down from the Abyssinian plateau during the annual floods of the Nile. For the farmers of the Nile throughout history, the greatest problems occurred not when the river flooded, but when it failed to flood, thus denying Egypt the life-giving waters necessary to nourish its crops, such as cotton, grain and sugar cane, in the otherwise arid sands.

Indeed, when the Egyptians in recent years attempted to harness the Nile by

At Ur in Mesopotamia, workmen stand before an exposed eight-foot layer of clay left by a flood of the Euphrates around 3200 B.C. So extensive was this deluge that ancient man may have believed that it, like Noah's flood, enveloped the entire earth.

Archeologist C. Leonard Woolley (*foreground, second from left*), his associates and Arab workmen gaze over an excavated Mesopotamian burial pit in 1929. Woolley and four assistants, with 180 local workers, uncovered an area 200 feet across, then decided to sink shafts below the deepest level to probe for artifacts from an even earlier time.

In March 1929, archeologists the world over were electrified by an announcement in *The Times* of London that a British colleague, C. Leonard Woolley, had uncovered evidence of the Biblical Deluge at an excavation in Mesopotamia near the Euphrates River. He had made his discovery while digging into a Sumerian burial pit from 3500 B.C.

The workers had gone down 40 feet when they announced that they had reached virgin soil. The material proved to be water-deposited clay and was devoid of artifacts. But Woolley sensed that he had not yet reached the beginnings of civilization in the area and had his men keep digging.

The barren clay flood deposits were eight feet thick; underneath, the soil was again studded with artifacts of an earlier, entirely different, pre-Sumerian culture. The layer of alluvial clay marked the abrupt end of one civilization and the beginning of another. The event matched the Bible's description of how the waters covered the land, and "all flesh that moved on the earth died." Concluded Woolley: "We had thus found the Flood on which is based the story of Noah."

building a great dam across the river, the engineers unwittingly disturbed an essential part of nature's great balancing act. The effects on the ecosystem of the River Nile and its valley were unforeseen—and in some ways unfortunate.

The series of events that results in a flood begins when raindrops strike the earth's surface and spatter in miniature explosions of moisture. The surface itself has been compared to a sieve placed under a faucet. If the screen is coarse, water passes rapidly through; if the mesh is fine and the tap is opened wide, some water gets through but the rest slowly rises until the sieve overflows.

Just so with rain water. If the soil in an area is composed of coarse sand or gravel, the rain water is quickly absorbed. But if clay, with its fine, closely adhering particles, is present, then not much water filters through and all the rest either evaporates or runs off into streams. Of all surfaces, the least permeable—and therefore the most likely to produce severe runoff and subsequent flooding—are those created by humans in their urban developments. When spread across the soil, such substances as concrete and asphalt act as shields against infiltration—and seemingly harmless little streams can suddenly become deadly torrents.

Throughout most of its innocuous life, Four Mile Run (a misnomer, since it is just under nine miles long) was nothing more than a quiet creek, easy to wade at any point of its course through the countryside of northern Virginia, just across the Potomac River from Washington, D.C. Four jurisdictions intersect within the stream's 19-square-mile drainage basin: Arlington and Fairfax Counties, and the cities of Falls Church and Alexandria. About 70 per cent of the basin (13 square miles) lies in a part of Arlington County that was largely rural 40 years ago.

But the years after World War II brought a building boom to the region. Home builders and commercial developers swarmed onto the scene, and open spaces surrendered to an onslaught of single-family houses. Shopping centers and apartment buildings also sprang up with broad expanses of paved parking lots, and schools were constructed with hard-surfaced playgrounds. Narrow road and railroad bridges impeded the free flow of the stream—a problem exacerbated by the dumping of society's discards, such as splintered lumber, broken cinder blocks, mattresses, worn-out tires, even cars. Highways, roads and sidewalks crisscrossed Four Mile Run's drainage basin; an estimated 85 per cent of the basin was developed and almost 40 per cent of the land was covered.

Under these circumstances, it was inevitable that Four Mile Run would flood disastrously, and in 1963 the stream finally rebelled. On August 20, after heavy rains, the stream surged over its banks, killing only one person but damaging 150 houses, 134 apartments and 31 business establishments. The total damage was estimated at $1.5 million. Within a month the U.S. Army Corps of Engineers, which is responsible for most of the nation's flood-control work, responded to calls for action by initiating a study of ways to curb the obstreperous stream.

The peace was shattered again in 1967, and in 1969 when Four Mile Run flooded not once but twice, both times causing sufficient damage to qualify the regions most seriously affected as disaster areas for purposes of federal aid. By now it was fairly commonplace for residents to be rescued by rowboat from the rooftops where they had sought refuge. On one occasion, the fact that a bridge was underwater prevented firemen from reaching an inundated shopping center where a blaze had broken out. Another time a traffic officer, unable to leave the area, rushed to a nearby telephone booth to call for help; by the time he left the booth, he had to swim for his life. In 1972, floods caused by Hurricane Agnes brought $14 million of damage to the area. Incredibly, this figure was surpassed in 1975 when flood losses in the wake of Hurricane Heloise amounted to more than $19 million.

A few years before, the Corps of Engineers had come up with a construction plan it estimated would cost about $10 million. The project entailed such measures as building levees and flood walls, widening the channel in the downstream area and replacing road and railroad bridges. Congressional approval of the project was contingent upon the adoption of a Watershed Management Program—the first of its kind in the United States—for the entire Four Mile Run basin. The plan required developers to build facilities to help regulate runoff during heavy rains. Work began in 1974 and, except for removing silt from the new channel, was finished in 1980. The final cost was $64 million—more than six times the original estimate.

Just as virtually watertight urban construction greatly increases runoff, so vegetation impedes it. Raindrops are trapped on leaf surfaces, sometimes long enough for evaporation to take place before there is any significant runoff. In heavily wooded areas or grasslands, light showers may be almost entirely intercepted by vegetation and returned to the atmosphere before reaching the ground. Moreover, the roots of trees and other plants (as well as animal burrows and the minuscule corridors created by worms) cause fissures in the surface soil that may help water to infiltrate. On the other hand, rapid runoff and consequent flooding can be expected in areas that have been denuded of their vegetation by fire, by grazing or by the feckless felling of trees.

Thus, the combination of soil characteristics and vegetation type and density largely determines the infiltration rate of water. If the infiltration rate is one inch per hour and two inches of rain fall within that period, then the extra inch (less the amount that evaporates) runs off into streams. Another element also enters into the equation: No matter how fast or how freely water infiltrates the surface, it is very likely to seep down to a layer of less permeable rock. As rain continues over a period of time, the water level above the rock layer—known as the water table—may rise until it overflows onto the surface. Then it, too, becomes runoff.

Such water exerts tremendous force. An inch of rainfall descending 1,000 feet and draining one square mile has the energy potential of 60,000 tons of TNT, or three times the force of the original Hiroshima nuclear bomb. Once this energy enters a stream it is captured within a channel that acts as a natural conduit and concentrates it into a brutal battering ram.

Even in the most placid of times, the passage of water downstream is a surprisingly turbulent one. As a river enters a bend, it often becomes a seething mass within which the individual particles of water, buffeted from outer to inner bank, now dipping and now rising, surge in a generally corkscrew motion that is disrupted by countless swirls and boils and eddies.

The velocity of a river is largely determined by gravity: The greater the volume of water and the steeper the grade, the faster it goes. But the friction of the earth's surface beneath, of the air above, and even within the water itself imposes a speed limit; water in a channel cannot move overland at more than about 20 miles per hour. Still, considering the fantastic forces involved, that would be enough to spell calamity for almost anything that gets in its way.

Hydrologists—those scientists who specialize in the behavior of water compute that the force of water increases as the square of the velocity. Thus the force of a river is four times greater at 10 miles per hour than at 5 miles per hour; at 20 miles per hour it is 16 times greater than it is at 5. But because of the very nature of turbulence, the speed, and therefore the force, of a river may be significantly more or less than the average from one place to the next. The force of running water is so great that a person would find it difficult to stand in a river only three feet deep and flowing at an apparently sluggish two miles per hour. As the depth and volume of water increase, so does the momentum of the water—at even slower speeds.

As it moves, water digs at the interstices between soil particles, dislodging

Nature's Great Hydrologic Cycle

Since the beginning of time billions of years ago, when the first clouds formed and the first rains fell, the water of the earth's environment has been in perpetual motion. Over and over again, the same water is conveyed from the earth's surface to the atmosphere and back with little ever lost or gained.

This pattern of never-ending circulation is known as the hydrologic cycle, and just as the human body's circulatory system sustains and distributes lifeblood, this natural pumping and distillation process sustains and distributes the earth's water supply. Solar energy and the relentless tug of the earth's own gravity fuel the cycle and keep the water moving.

As illustrated in the diagram at right, water vapor enters the atmosphere by evaporation from bodies of water and by transpiration from plants and trees. Scientists calculate that every year a fantastic 10 million billion (one and 16 zeroes) gallons of water is carried aloft in this manner. An estimated 86 per cent comes from the oceans, which contain about 97 per cent of the earth's total water resources; another 12 per cent comes from rivers, lakes and streams; and the remaining 2 per cent is the result of transpiration from vegetation.

Once aloft, the moisture cools and collects into clouds as it rises higher into the atmosphere. When temperature and moisture content reach the proper stage the vapor in the clouds condenses, and the water in these airborne reservoirs falls to the earth as rain or snow.

Once returned to the surface, the water may evaporate again rapidly, or it may soak down into the earth and remain as groundwater for thousands of years until at last it again finds its way to an outlet. But regardless of where the precipitation falls, or how long it remains, eventually it is recycled.

At any given moment, only about .005 per cent of the earth's estimated 326 million cubic miles of water is actively involved in the hydrologic cycle. And because of fluctuations in the grand atmospheric scheme of things, the actual amount of water available to various regions of the world can vary dramatically, often bringing searing drought or devastating flood.

TRANSPIRATION

EVAPORATION

SNOW

RAIN

LAKE

GROUNDWATER

The East and West Lyn Rivers, after a devastating flash flood in August 1952, course along the new channel they cut through the middle of the Devonshire resort village of Lynmouth. During the restoration of the town, the hotel at left was leveled in order to accommodate the dredging and widening of the boulder-strewn waterway.

them and then swirling them along with the current in a process known as entrainment. The carrying capacities of moving water increase proportionately with velocity and, correspondingly, with turbulence. Assuming a more or less smooth bed, a large river flowing at about half a mile per hour can entrain very fine particles, such as sand-sized lignite; to transport the heavier grains of quartz sand along that same smooth bed would require a current of nearly one mile per hour.

Not only does water flow faster than one mile per hour on a steep grade, but the entrained materials themselves move much more readily downhill. Floodwaters rushing and roaring down a precipitous slope can perform prodigious feats of transportation, sweeping along enormous boulders that roll and slide and bounce as they go, adding their own destructive weight to the force of the water. In August 1952, to its great misfortune, the little town of Lynmouth, England, lay in the path of such a flood. What happened to Lynmouth stands as an extreme example of how steep terrain and heavy rain may combine to reshape the land.

The quaint seaside village (Lynmouth derives its name from an old Anglo-Saxon term meaning "the town on the torrent"), with its thatch-roofed cottages and superb surrounding scenery, was once a place of repose for poets. Percy Bysshe Shelley dwelt there for a year and his contemporary Robert Southey left a loving description of the topography that would one day bring calamity. "Two rivers join at Lynmouth," he wrote. "Each of these flows down a combe rolling over huge stones like a long waterfall. From the hill between the two is a prospect most magnificent."

More specifically, Lynmouth sits in a narrow Y-shaped valley at the confluence of the West and East Lyn Rivers in north Devon. Draining 39 square miles of the high, heather-covered plateau—the Chains of Exmoor—the two streams funnel through oak-forested gorges, plunging some 1,500 feet in four miles before joining for a short final lunge to the sea.

Lynmouth has a year-round population of about 450, but during the summer of 1952 about 750 tourists had come to bask on the nearby beach or to roam the heathered hillsides. They had been having a soggy time of it; during the first two weeks of August, intermittent but often heavy rain soaked the entire area, saturating the earth and diminishing its capacity to absorb more water. Friday,

A ruined house awaiting demolition in the wake of the Lynmouth flood reflects the fury of the water's overnight onslaught. Nearly 100 homes were destroyed, and losses were estimated at two million dollars, yet the townspeople, with the help of Royal Army Engineers, were able to reopen Lynmouth to tourists only one month later.

August 15, was an especially dismal day. Rain fell from a leaden sky, and even at midday the lights were on in most houses. In the afternoon, at least one sky-gazer noted an eerie and ominous sight: A sullen cloud bank, black but bruised by dark reds and purples, moved very slowly from west to east; beneath it a layer of clouds appeared to race swiftly in the opposite direction. A torrential rain was soon falling on the area. By evening the East and West Lyns were swollen and turbulent.

At around 6:30 p.m., after a brief lull, the rain redoubled in its intensity, sluicing down in suffocating sheets. In the next five hours, it was later estimated, more than six inches fell on Lynmouth and the surrounding uplands, for a total of nine inches in a 24-hour period. At about 7:30 p.m., the canal carrying water to Lynmouth's hydroelectric station was overwhelmed by the racing waters, and the plant went dead. An emergency diesel system was switched on to provide Lynmouth with light. At 9 p.m. the backup system, its engine fly-wheels flooded, was shut down. Lynmouth lay in darkness, the night's silence shattered by the roar of rushing water.

The electrical failure brought an untimely end to a local variety show being held in the Lynmouth Pavilion. Upon leaving, members of the audience were dismayed to find that the roads were already submerged. Most sought safety on nearby Mars Hill. But seven determined ladies linked their arms and sloshed intrepidly up Lynmouth Street toward the Lyn Valley Hotel. On the left and nearest to the crumbling riverbank was Elsie Cherry, a 56-year-old Londoner. Suddenly, Miss Cherry slipped and was swallowed by the surging water. Her body was found weeks later at Clovelly, more than 30 miles away. The others were lucky enough to scramble to safety.

Above Lynmouth, a small group of homes backed onto a ravine; the West Lyn normally ran 30 feet below. In one of these lived Thomas Floyd, 63, a district councilor, with his invalid wife and five other family members; also there on that fatal night were two rain-soaked travelers from Durham, who had been given shelter. Soon after 9:30, Floyd's 27-year-old son, Fred, alarmed by the tumult outside, looked out the kitchen window and shouted: "Water is coming down the back garden and the wall is breaking." Thomas Floyd later recalled: "Our first thoughts were that we must get mother out of the house. We were trying to get her up from the bed when the water came pouring in, and without any warning the house toppled over."

Floyd managed to seize a section of brickwork that had somehow remained standing; he survived. But the eight others who had been in the house perished that night.

During the hours of horror at the peak of the flood, an estimated 575 tons of water raged down the gorges of the East and West Lyns every second, at times forming a wall 30 feet high, churning up and sweeping with it great boulders, tearing out the stone bridges that had been so much a part of Lynmouth's charm. Lynmouth was, quite simply, demolished. The next morning much of the village and the shoreline lay buried beneath about 200,000 tons of boulders, some weighing 15 tons apiece. That night 93 houses were either swept away or irreparably damaged; 132 vehicles were washed out to sea. Thirty-four people lost their lives, and officials still suspect that some holidaymakers may have died and never been accounted for.

But good fortune also played a hand. It was a close call, for example, for the Lyndale Hotel's 60 occupants, who raced the rising waters to the top floor of the building. Next day those survivors left their haven by stepping through a top-floor window onto a carpet of boulders that lay piled high outside.

Beyond Lynmouth, the beaches were strewn for miles with debris of every description—splintered lumber, broken telegraph poles, twisted steel girders, smashed cars, and many thousands of saplings that had been uprooted and stripped of their bark by the grinding action of the flood.

To rate floods on a statistical basis, hydrologists use a rather simple—at least in its concept—system. Depending on the records of a given river's past performances, a particular inundation may be classified as, say, a 10-year or a 100-year flood—meaning that a flood of that magnitude may, on the average, be expected every 10 or every 100 years. This does not, of course, mean that the floods are neatly spaced at regular 10- or 100-year intervals. The Mississippi, for example, experienced 100-year floods in 1943, 1944, 1947 and 1951. What the system does do is assess the chances of a 100-year flood occurring in any specific year at roughly 1 in 100.

Although the nightmare in Lynmouth cannot be rated in this way—there are no systematic records of the discharge of the Lyn Rivers—hydrologists have called it a 50,000-year flood, ranking it, hypothetically at least, among England's most severe.

Such floods require rare circumstances indeed, but it is possible for inundations expected more frequently to wreak even greater havoc. Heavy rainfall, an early snow thawed suddenly by a warm wind, hardpan clay, a dearth of vegetation, steep hills in the watershed, a river flowing down a significant grade, narrow city streets and alleys in which the flooding water is caged like a wild beast, centuries of past human complacency, and blunders during moments of present crisis—all these are the ingredients of potential catastrophe. In November 1966 they combined to bring ruin to *Firenze Bella—Beautiful Florence—*the home of Renaissance man and the cradle of modern Western culture.

Elizabeth Barrett Browning, using her full quota of poetic license, once described the Arno River, which bisects Florence, as "this crystal arrow in the gentle sunset." More accurately, the Arno is a dirty brown stream that runs a short course of 150 miles from its source in the Apennines to its exit into the Mediterranean. During a dry season, the Arno is little more than a mud flat; even when the river is at its normal stage, fishermen can wade almost to the middle of the stream to cast their lines. At Florence, after draining the hills lining the Casentino valley and before leveling out for its final push through a broad flood plain toward Pisa, the Arno flows downgrade between 25-foot embankments, the northern one topped by a four-foot wall of concrete and brick—which is just about the only concession the Florentines have ever made to flood control.

That is very strange, since the Arno, despite its deceptively sluggish appearance, has been a threat for centuries. In the days of the Etruscans, from 800 to 100 B.C., the hills of the river's watershed were lush with oak, beech, pine and chestnut forests. As late as 300 B.C. Roman military forces avoided the area because the deep woods provided perfect cover for ambush by local defenders. But as Florence became a population center, the trees were hacked down to provide timber for building. The hills were never adequately reforested; their naked clay formed an almost impermeable surface, and rain water rushed in sheets down the steep slopes.

The first recorded flood of the Arno took place in 1117 A.D., when high water ripped out the Ponte Vecchio, then the only span across the river at Florence. On November 4, 1333, a flood claimed 300 lives; an eyewitness named Giovanni Villani wrote: "In their houses people beat upon bowls and caldrons and cried to God 'misericordia, misericordia,' and people fled from house to house and roof to roof and made such noise and tumult that the thunder itself could scarce be heard."

Between 1500 and 1510 Leonardo da Vinci submitted plans for a complex diversion of the Arno involving a large retention basin, a canal, a tunnel and floodgates to bring the river under control. His plans were ignored, and Leonardo contented himself by writing a nephew a letter warning against living in Florence's low-lying Santa Croce district, which the great man deemed especially vulnerable to the Arno's incursions. Leonardo was prescient. In 1547 the river again broke into Florence, causing more than 100 deaths and devastating Santa Croce.

In morose contemplation of that disaster, one Bernardo Segni pointed to a major cause. "Because very great numbers of trees had been cut down for timber in the Falterona and other mountains," he wrote, "the soil was more easily loosened by water and carried down to silt up the beds of rivers. In these ways man had contributed to the disaster."

Despite repeated warnings and despite major floods that continued for centuries at a rate of one every 26 years, Florence was singularly unprepared for the dark events of November 3-4, 1966. The upper valley of the Arno held steep rocky ravines—perfect funnels for heavy rains; the hills in the middle reaches

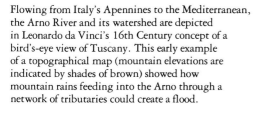

Flowing from Italy's Apennines to the Mediterranean, the Arno River and its watershed are depicted in Leonardo da Vinci's 16th Century concept of a bird's-eye view of Tuscany. This early example of a topographical map (mountain elevations are indicated by shades of brown) showed how mountain rains feeding into the Arno through a network of tributaries could create a flood.

remained largely bare of cover, their lower slopes densely populated, and two dams had been built upstream of Florence, not for flood control, but to furnish hydroelectric power. Never in the river's history had any serious attempt been made to deepen its bed by dredging. Perhaps most thoughtless of all, many of the world's greatest art treasures and rarest manuscripts were kept in basements—sure prey for hungry waters.

October had been wet, with rain falling day after dreary day, stirring the Arno from its customary torpor. November, however, began with two clear, crisp days, offering hope for fair weather on the 4th, when a national holiday would celebrate the end of World War I, in which Italy had been among the victorious Allies. November 3 ended that pleasant prospect with a blinding downpour; during the 48 hours of November 3-4, Florence and the Arno watershed would receive 19 inches—more than one third of the area's average annual rainfall.

Late on November 3, events occurred upstream that though they were by no means the primary cause of Florence's ensuing tragedy, surely contributed to it. Despite a subsequent government investigation, the details remain unclear amid a welter of denials and charges and countercharges. It appears, however, that the operators of the Penna hydroelectric dam, 29 miles from Florence, having failed to release water gradually during the preceding weeks of heavy rainfall, now let loose a huge mass, thereby placing an impossible burden on the Levane hydroelectric dam, just four miles downstream and 25 miles from Florence. At that facility, already brim full, the engineers in charge soon faced a

A map of Florence shows the distribution of the Arno's 1966 floodwaters. The worst inundation —up to 20 feet of water and mud—occurred in the low-lying Santa Croce district and in two pockets to its south *(dark blue).* Six to 12 feet collected on slightly higher ground surrounding Piazza Beccaria *(light blue),* while in the remainder of Florence within one mile of the river the water reached depths of up to six feet *(purple).*

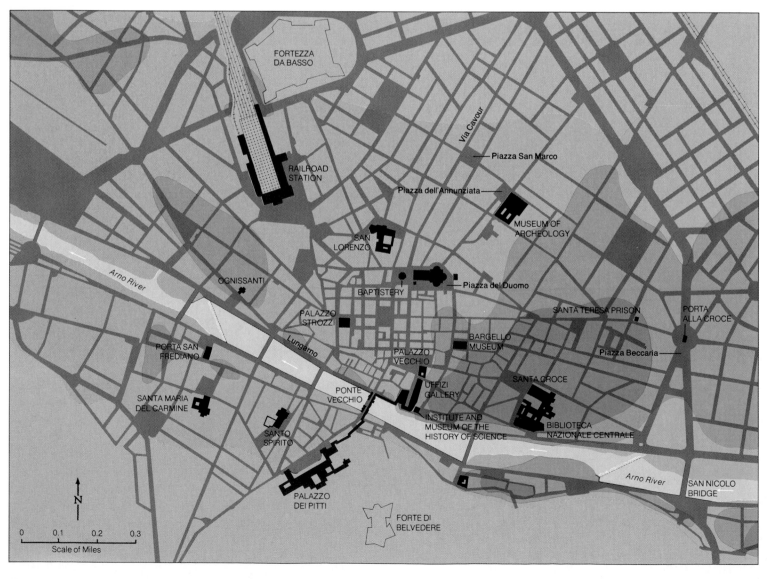

terrible decision. At 9 p.m., Signora Ida Raffaelli, who lived below the Levane edifice, heard a blast of the siren used to give warning that water was about to be released. "I was appalled to see the gates slowly opening," she said later, "and immediately an enormous wall of water started coming down the Arno toward us. I screamed to my sister and we ran for our lives."

There is an old Florentine saying that "the Arno will not flood until the Sieve fills its cup." And now the Sieve tributary, ordinarily a peaceful little stream entering the Arno a few miles below the Levane Dam, added its swollen burden to the waters already raging down the river.

Some Florentines recall having retired early, unknowing and unworried, on that dismal night. One who did not was Romildo Cesaroni, an elderly night watchman whose job it was to patrol on his bicycle the goldsmith and jewelry shops lining the Ponte Vecchio, which had been rebuilt after the great flood of 1333. Cesaroni had been watching the Arno for many years, but he had never before seen it rise so rapidly. Shortly after midnight, with the water rushing only three feet beneath the bridge (it normally flowed more than 20 feet lower), he began to telephone the owners of the shops in his care.

Among those who heeded the old watchman's summons were jeweler Tebaldo Piccini-Risaliti and his wife, who seized several suitcases and hurried to the Ponte Vecchio to try to save their most precious wares. Within the shop, Signora Piccini-Risaliti recalled, "the floor was shaking terribly under our feet, and outside I could see tree trunks looking as if they were going to crash in through the window. We collected up some more things, but then the bridge started shaking so violently that we thought it was going to collapse at any moment, and we ran for it." Remarkably, the ancient Ponte Vecchio held, along with all the city's other bridges.

Around 3 a.m., a reporter for the newspaper *Nazione* called the city's water processing plant to check on the condition of the aqueduct. He was answered by a 52-year-old night-shift employee named Carlo Maggiorelli, who had come on duty at 8 p.m. "It's a shambles," Maggiorelli reported. "Everything's going under." Despite the newsman's urging that he leave, Maggiorelli insisted on remaining at his post. His body was recovered two days later, buried in mud.

By now the city's antiquated sewer system, built over three centuries begin-

Part of an irreplaceable collection of a million books from the Biblioteca Nazionale Centrale soaked by the Florence flood dries on 50-foot-high tobacco racks. Truckloads of sodden books were hauled to tobacco barns, pottery kilns and textile plants to be dried at high temperatures, then treated for mildew. Most of the volumes survived intact and eventually were returned to the library and the State Archives.

ning in 1569, when Tuscany was still a grand duchy, had given way before the tremendous pressure of river water backing into it; human waste gushed out of manholes; the stench permeated Florence. The constant honking of parked cars, their electrical systems shorted by rain water, shared in a weird cacophony with the pathetic howls of watchdogs trapped within warehouse fences.

The Arno broke into the low-lying south-bank districts of Gavinana and San Frediano, where dwelt many of Florence's poorest citizens. There died the old and the helpless—an 81-year-old man, a 71-year-old pensioner, a 74-year-old and his 52-year-old wife.

Next the Arno burst through the low wall on the north bank, pouring onto streets laid out some 700 years before and collectively known as the Lungarno (meaning "along the Arno") in Florence's Old Town. On one of those dark and narrow passages Dante had been plunged into despair by a snub from his be-

A statue of the Virgin Mary stands forlornly amid the thick deposits of slime and muck left by floodwaters in Florence's Basilica of Santa Croce. At the height of the flood the water in this 13th Century Franciscan church was 20 feet deep.

loved Beatrice; in one of the Old Town's many small piazzas, the fire had been made ready for Savonarola's ordeal. Now, throughout that hallowed district, the flood churned implacably, a slimy mass made thick by 500,000 tons of silt washed down from the naked hills. Already the sound of explosions could be heard as furnaces and fuel storage tanks ruptured and released millions of gallons of the oil that would transform the roiling floodwater into sludge and leave its malign mark on everything it touched.

A rain-soaked dawn came at 6 a.m., and Kathrine Kressmann Taylor, an American writer living in Florence, peered at the Arno from a window of her *pensione* and beheld "a snarling brown torrent of terrific velocity, spiraling in whirlpools and countercurrents that send waves running backward. This tremendous water carries mats of debris: straw, twigs, leafy branches, rags, a litter that the river sucks down and spews up again in a swelling turbulence."

At about 7 a.m. the whispered matins in the great Church of Ognissanti were interrupted by a shout of *"L'Arno è fuori!"* ("The Arno is out!"). The 17 Franciscan priests and brothers inside the church secured the front doors with an iron bar and worked desperately to move precious paraphernalia to the elevated altar. Then, unable to withstand the power of the water crashing against the doors, the bar broke. Recalled Ognissanti's guardian, Father Costantino: "It was as though a huge and angry giant had smashed his way in." Another priest, Father Pietro, tried to fight his way to the doors to close them and was knocked from his feet. He saved himself by grabbing and holding on to the end of a cane held out to him by a colleague—even as the water poured down the nave and reached toward Botticelli's 15th Century fresco *Saint Augustine,* completely soaking its lower portion.

At precisely 7:26 a.m., every electric clock in Florence stopped—and for the next 24 hours the city was without power. The full force of the flood was upon the city. The San Nicolo Bridge, easternmost of seven, was underwater; in Gavinana the water was six feet deep. Roads leading out of the city were blocked in all directions, railroad tracks were covered. Florentines had no choice but to stay where they were.

The cavernous 13th Century church of Santa Croce was filled with 15 feet of water that swirled over the tombs containing the dust of Michelangelo, Galileo, Rossini and Machiavelli. In the museum next door, the oily tide daubed Cimabue's 14-foot *Crucifix,* venerated for nearly 700 years. In the basement stacks of the Biblioteca Nazionale Centrale, Italy's largest library, more than one million books and manuscripts were soaked and smeared. At the Baptistery in the Piazza del Duomo, five of Ghiberti's 10 magnificent bronze panels of Old Testament scenes were torn from the portals that Michelangelo had called the "Doors of Paradise." At the Institute and Museum of the History of Science, Director Maria Luisa Righini-Bonelli 28 times edged perilously along a third-floor ledge to the adjacent Uffizi Gallery. She saved about 35 precious objects—including several of Galileo's telescopes.

In Florence's Santa Teresa prison, water rose to a depth of 13 feet, and prisoners were herded to the top floor—where they overpowered their guards. About 80 convicts climbed to the prison's roof. As they huddled there, people stranded on the rooftops of nearby houses urged them to try to escape. "Go on, jump!" shouted one. "There's a tree trunk just coming." A young prisoner named Luciano Sonnellini hesitated, then leaped, grasping frantically for the onrushing tree. He missed—and his corpse was later found in a cellar nearly a mile away.

Before dawn just outside the city, at the race track behind Cascine Park, stable hands, owners and trainers had struggled for three hours to load 270 horses into vans before the floodwaters arrived. Finally forced to flee, they left behind them 70 of the terrified animals. A few days later their carcasses were burned with flame throwers to prevent the spread of disease.

The rain continued throughout the day without sign of slackening. At about 6 p.m. a government delegation from Rome managed to get into the nearly isolated city. "Behind a curtain of driving rain, pierced here and there by dim, mysterious lights, the Piazza San Marco was a storm-tossed lake," wrote *Nazione* editor Enrico Mattei, a member of the group. "This lake was fed by a violent torrent which poured down from the Piazza dell'Annunziata, lapped at the church and went swirling off down the Via Cavour in the direction of the Cathedral. Beneath the grim rumbling of the water, we could hear a subdued murmur of human voices."

Some of that sound came from about 100,000 persons who had been marooned on upper floors and on rooftops, where they remained throughout the horrid night of November 4. For those frightened souls, wrote Kathrine Taylor, it was "a night out of the Middle Ages, without light, with no help available during the black hours, no voice to answer a cry. The people who are clinging to the ridges of their roofs cannot see the water rising in the dark, they can only dread it, and feel the rain pour down."

The following morning the sky was clear, the sun shining and the flood receding. One of the first things that Kathrine Taylor saw when she emerged from her *pensione* was a porter trying with an old broom to sweep away an ocean of mud from the entrance of a palace nearby. The resurrection of Florence had already begun.

Long ago a goldsmith named Bernardo Cennini had pridefully said of his people: "Nothing is beyond the powers of the Florentines." But in 1966, the Florentines needed help—which they received in abundance. Hardly had the

The most highly valued casualty of the 1966 Florence flood, the pre-Renaissance wooden *Crucifix* by Giovanni Cimabue clearly shows the ravages of its submersion in these before-and-after pictures. After 10 years of painstaking labor—involving retrieval of missing chips of paint from the mud-covered floor of the museum of Santa Croce and removal of the rest of the paint to permit thorough drying of the underlying wood—experts were able to restore a portion of the masterpiece's former beauty.

skies cleared when the first contingents of students from 10 European countries, and from the United States and Brazil, arrived on the scene. For three weeks, hundreds of them toiled at recovering more than a million books from the slime of the Biblioteca Nazionale Centrale; many wore gas masks against the overwhelming odor of sewage and the rotting leather of the books' bindings. Scores of students who had been studying in Florence formed a human chain at the State Archives and retrieved some 40,000 volumes. Because they almost uniformly wore blue jeans, they became known to grateful Florentines as the Blue Angels. From the United States and Europe flew planeloads of the world's leading Renaissance scholars, art historians and restoration experts.

Ghiberti's priceless panels were found buried in muck and were returned to their proper place on the Doors of Paradise. Michelangelo's statues, given a thick coating of talcum to draw out moisture and oil, then treated with powerful detergents to erase the flood's stains, survived hardly the worse for wear.

But although restoration experts and the Santa Croce monks worked on their hands and knees, sifting through the mud in search of tiny bits of color flaked from Cimabue's *Crucifix,* the great painting was largely destroyed. In the Church of Ognissanti, the *Saint Augustine* fresco was removed from the wall, cleaned, dried and reapplied to a portable wall support. Donatello's 500-year-old sculpture in wood of Mary Magdalene was painstakingly cleaned, using liquid solvents and surgical lancets; remarkably, it is now in better condition than before the flood. Fifteen years after the flood, more than 500,000 of the one million damaged books at the Biblioteca Nazionale Centrale had been cleaned and in many cases rebound, as had 23,000 of 110,000 swamped volumes in the Gabinetto Vissieux in the Palazzo Strozzi—a repository of 19th and 20th Century works. And the work was still going on. The Museum of Archeology's incomparable Etruscan collection was badly damaged, although about 30,000 other objects were repaired.

Still, in one sense, the Florentines were fortunate. Though many thousands were made homeless and hundreds injured, only 35 persons had died in the Arno's terrible flood. Ω

Chapter 2

THE YELLOW RIVER: CHINA'S SORROW

Spreading like a gigantic fan across more than 125,000 square miles of North China, the flat and featureless expanse of the Great Plain appeared to an observer in 1917 to be studded by thousands of small earthen mounds that covered the shallow graves of countless generations. As floodwaters poured over the plain, the soil washed from the graves and wooden coffins were set afloat like tiny boats—with skeletons as their macabre passengers, ghostly symbols of the intimate, age-old relationship between man and flood.

Upon this enormous plain formed almost entirely by river sediments, it is probable that more humans have lived and died than in any other place of similar size on earth. One educated estimate puts the number at more than one trillion. Here was the cradle of Chinese civilization, with archeological evidence of activities as far back as 500,000 years; and here today dwell upward of 120 million people, tilling the 50 million acres that constitute about 20 per cent of the ancient nation's cultivated land. "Here the whole of life and the whole of death take place on the inherited ground," wrote Count Hermann Keyserling, a 1912 traveler on the North China Plain. "Man belongs to the soil, not the soil to man; it will never let its children go."

Snaking across the vast flatland is what appears from a distance to be a colossal, elevated roadway. It is in fact the Yellow River, confined by dikes 100 feet wide at their bases, 50 feet at their crests and 30 feet high to imprison a stream whose bed, built up by the world's heaviest load of silt, runs in some places 15 feet above the level of the North China Plain.

During its turbulent history and at various points along its lengthy course, the Yellow has been known by at least 80 different nicknames, including the Ungovernable, the Scourge of the Sons of Han and, most commonly, China's Sorrow. By whatever name, it has claimed more lives and caused more human suffering than any other single natural feature on the earth's face. Throughout the ages, Chinese engineers have worked unceasingly to control the Yellow; their labors are legendary, and the men themselves are revered as folk heroes. Yet despite all the herculean efforts past and present, the Yellow River during the last 3,500 years has torn through or surged over its restricting dikes no fewer than 1,500 times to bring catastrophe to large parts of China's Great Plain. And less than a century ago the river was responsible for one of the worst natural disasters known to history.

In its 2,878-mile length the Yellow ranks fourth among the rivers of the world—nearly 200 miles longer than Africa's Congo, but more than 1,000 miles shorter than South America's Amazon. In the average volume of its flow it is far down the list, about on a par with North America's Arkansas River. But

Yü, the legendary founder of China's dynastic system 4,000 years ago, is best remembered by modern-day Chinese for his efforts to control the flood-prone Yellow River. According to Chinese lore, Yü, the "Son of Heaven," was commissioned by Emperor Shun to tame the waters and drive out the serpents and dragons, thus making the flood plain habitable.

in its killing floods, the Yellow River stands alone—thanks largely to the far-reaching alluvial plain that offers little or no topographic haven to the terrified peasants who flee the muddy waters.

As one of nature's relentless forces, here wearing down the land, there building it up, rivers create flood plains in their lower reaches. The formation of a flood plain results from the behavior of water running within channels and periodically spilling over their banks; the volume, the speed and turbulence of flow, and the amount and type of sediment being carried are all factors in the creation of the plain. As every free-flowing river leaves the mountains or hills in its upper and middle reaches, its course becomes a succession of sweeping bends known as meanders. While traveling through its twisting channel, the water has a tendency to erode the outer, or concave, bank of a meander; at the same time, the slower-moving current on the inner, or convex, bank deposits sediment. Streams, therefore, continuously migrate across their valleys, cutting into concave banks and building onto convex ones—all the while remaining much the same in width. In this manner, a flood plain is formed on both sides of a river.

Rivers in flood make special sedimentary contributions to their plains. When a river tops its natural banks, or for that matter man-made levees, water laps over the crests in thin sheets. Velocity is almost immediately checked by friction and by loss of volume—and sedimentation starts, with the heavier materials settling first and the finer particles later. If the water's escape has been violent, as when a river rips open a breach in its dikes, the entrained materials may be carried farther from the stream, but the sequence of deposition remains the same.

Just as with other rivers, the Yellow constantly builds a flood plain along its lower course. But the Yellow is exceptional, for unlike most rivers, it dumps phenomenal quantities of silt, especially during floods, in its channel and along its banks. And further, unlike the flood plains of many other rivers, that of the Yellow is unconstrained by surrounding topography, so that the greatest floods can result in a radical change of course for the river, and the subsequent creation of a new flood plain. A constant, albeit irregular, cycle of floods and course changes has thus enabled the Yellow to coat a vast area of North China's alluvial plain with sand and silt.

A variety of geologic factors dictates the damage caused by a flooding river, and even during a great flood, very few rivers will, like the Yellow, escape completely and for extended periods the confines of their channels. China's Yangtze, for example, normally carries 18 times as much water as its Yellow sister. Yet during much of its course the Yangtze rushes through spectacular gorges; in 1871 it rose by a staggering 275 feet within its walls downstream from Chungking, and when it subsided it left a river steamer perched 120 feet high on a jut of rock. In its lower reach the Yangtze cuts through a broad plain, where floods can be murderous. But they are relatively infrequent, thanks in part to two great lakes that are connected to the river by many channels and that act as reservoirs for Yangtze overflows.

By comparison, the Great Plain of the Yellow River is starkly and simply a deathtrap. China owes much of its eternal sorrow to the unique geology of the Yellow's middle reaches, the unreliable but periodically intense rainfall in its drainage basin and the nature of the alluvial North China Plain, upon whose fertile soils so many Chinese have depended for so long.

The Yellow is born as a clearwater stream that rises amid the swamps and lakes of the Tibetan highlands, more than 14,600 feet above sea level. During its journey of 1,000 miles to Kansu Province the seemingly harmless Yellow is less than 100 yards wide. In Kansu, the river picks up volume and velocity, rushing through no fewer than 16 precipitous gorges, evocative, but on a smaller scale, of Arizona's Grand Canyon. On this northern run the Yellow skirts the

A curious-looking stone levee bisects the Yellow as it meanders past an agricultural commune in China's arid Ningsia Province. The purpose of the midstream levee is twofold: to funnel water for irrigation into the two canals cut across the curves of the river and to reduce the undermining of the bank at left, where the commune is located. The peasants in the foreground are planting trees in the sandy dunes as part of an antierosion program.

How a river fashions a flood plain is illustrated at right. A young, relatively straight river (*top*) begins chiseling a snakelike channel by undercutting the banks of its outer curves and depositing silt on the opposite sides. As the river advances in age (*middle*), its winding path broadens the valley while silt deposits from periodic floods raise the valley floor. By the time the river reaches full maturity (*bottom*) it is characterized by sweeping bends and a zigzagging channel—and it has built up a broad flood plain that extends far beyond its banks.

Ordos Desert and penetrates beyond the Great Wall of China into Inner Mongolia before embarking on a 600-mile journey that takes it through one of the strangest lands on earth. In the early 1870s a German geologist, Baron Ferdinand von Richthofen, traveled through China's Shensi Province and marveled at what he saw. "Everything is yellow," he wrote. "The hills, the roads, the fields, the water of the rivers and brooks are yellow, the houses are made of yellow earth, the vegetation is covered with yellow dust. Even the atmosphere is seldom free from a yellow haze."

The pervasive coloration—which gives the Yellow River its name—is caused by what is known as loess, a German word used to describe silt deposits in the Rhine Valley that had been transported and deposited by the action of wind. In its reach southward, the Yellow, while slicing between Shansi and Shensi Provinces, passes through a vast loess plateau, 166,023 square miles blanketed to a depth of up to 450 feet by a tawny layer of loosely bound particles—a soil more susceptible to erosion than most other soils.

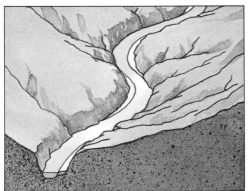

Geologists generally agree that the main source of the loess is the Gobi Desert in Mongolia, which has long since been stripped of its soil cover by wicked northwesterly winds, leaving bare, gravelly rock surfaces and occasional sand dunes. The wind-deposited loess in Shansi and Shenshi Provinces has been shaped by centuries of erosion into a tortured wilderness of grotesque landforms described by American author and Sino-expert Edgar Snow as "an infinite variety of queer, embattled shapes—hills like great castles, like ranges torn by some giant hand, leaving behind the imprint of angry fingers. Fantastic, incredible and sometimes frightening shapes, a world configurated by a mad God—and sometimes a world also of strange surrealist beauty."

Yet for all its forbidding appearance, the land of loess is surpassingly fertile, and more than 70 million people cultivate 35,000 square miles of the twisted terrain, depending for their existence on crops of wheat, millet, potatoes and apricots. From prehistory to the present, many of the inhabitants of the loessland have dwelt beneath their own farms, in caves dug either into the surface of the earth or into the steep faces of ravines. In places the landscape is almost devoid of structures. But along the edges of many fields rise plumes of smoke that escape through ventilating shafts from the heating and cooking fires below. The area is also largely empty of trees and other soil-binding natural vegetation; over the centuries, peasants in search of fuel and shelter have stripped away the forests of birch and pine on the hillsides and the cover of bushy artemisia on flatter ground.

As it traverses the loess plateau, the Yellow River entrains vast amounts of silt. And to this burden are added the gigantic loads carried by the Wei River and by the Fen and the K'uye Rivers, which join the Yellow after crossing the loessland; the K'uye, in fact, holds the distinction of being the planet's muddiest tributary—in one flood more than 90 per cent of its weight was silt. As a result, the Yellow is by a significant margin the world's siltiest river. Sediment amounting to 3 per cent of the total weight of a river's flow is considered high, and 10 per cent is rare. The silt carried by the Yellow at the time it leaves the loess plateau has been measured at as much as 46 per cent of the stream's weight—and in that astounding fact lies the crucial element of the river's lethal life.

The average annual load of the Yellow by the time it nears Meng-chin, the Honan Province gateway to the Great Plain, is 1.6 billion tons of silt—enough to encircle the entire globe 27 times with an earthen wall more than three feet high and three feet thick.

Upstream from Meng-chin, the average slope of the Yellow's course is about four feet in each mile, and the current is swift enough to keep nearly all the silt in transport. But below Meng-chin, where the river flows generally northeast for its 500-mile trip across the North China Plain to the sea, the average grade drops to 10 inches per mile. As the speed of the current slackens, the river deposits sediment so that only one quarter of the annual load is eventually discharged at the mouth of the Yellow. The rest, if evenly distributed inland, would cover more than 1,000 square miles with a foot of alluvium annually. It is, of course, distributed in no such fashion. Except during the most catastrophic floods, the sediment settles within the channel, on the adjacent flood plain or at the delta, which advances into the Po Sea at an incredible rate of nine square miles each year.

As the bed rises, so does the level of the stream, and the threat of flooding inevitably increases. To keep pace, humans throughout their span of time on the Great Plain have built dikes higher and higher along the elevated course of the Yellow River. And therein lies the rub.

Nearly 23 centuries before the birth of Christ, there was, according to Chinese legend, a monstrous Yellow River flood that lasted for 13 years. Ruling dynasties, blamed in the past for the river's rampages, had been toppled for floods of lesser magnitude, and after the failure of a court official named Kun to tame the torrent, Emperor Shun appointed Kun's son Yü to the job. He was given virtually unlimited human and material resources. Yü's principal flood-control effort was evidently directed at deepening the Yellow's channel by dredging. He also dug diversion canals in order to relieve the main stream of its heavy flow.

In time, after fantastic effort, Yü conquered the river, which according to the legend stayed docile for 1,600 years. For his triumph, Yü was made Emperor. He is still venerated in China as Yü the Great; "We should have been fish," the saying goes, "but for Yü."

Yü's success, if in fact it was anything more than legend, was unhappily transitory. Certainly by the Fifth Century B.C., the sophisticated methods of flood control attributed to him had been largely abandoned in favor of ritual mumbo jumbo and ceaseless building of dikes. In one district of the Yellow's watershed, priests and provincial officials required the annual sacrifice of a maiden to propitiate the river god. Adorned in ceremonial regalia, the victim was flung into the stream, where she was swiftly dragged beneath the surface by her heavy accouterments. Needless to say, the maiden was invariably selected from a peasant family rather than from the local gentry, and Chinese historians record that as the years passed, farmers who had eligible daughters deserted the district in increasing numbers. Eventually, around 400 B.C., a magistrate named Hsimen Pao stepped forth and put an end to the practice with one final, highly appropriate sacrifice: He had the priests and officials hurled to their deaths in the swirling yellow waters.

During the Han Dynasty, between 202 B.C. and 220 A.D., a unified system of dikes was adopted that improved flood control somewhat. Hitherto, the dikes had been built by groups of farmers or associations of villages intent on protecting only their own property. But under the Han Emperors, dike building was brought under a central authority, which worked to improve dike design and to organize labor more efficiently.

Han Dynasty successes were achieved largely because of orderly government. But during the following 2,000 years, as dynasty replaced dynasty, the pendulum swung back and forth between stability and instability. When peace and order prevailed, progress was made in curbing the Yellow. When society fell into disarray, so did efforts to control the river. Floods became more frequent—and increasingly catastrophic, as the number of people living on the Great Plain grew into the tens of millions.

The principal building material of the dikes was the very silt that the Yellow had transported from the loessland and deposited on the North China Plain. But since that soil had already demonstrated how easily it could be eroded,

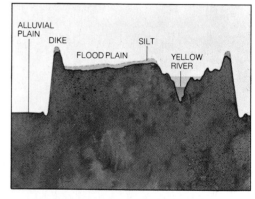

A cross section of the Yellow River illustrates the cycle that causes the river's bed and its protective dike system to grow higher and higher. As it flows toward the sea, the river continually deposits silt, which raises its bed and increases the threat of overtopping its natural banks. To compensate, the Chinese raise the level of the dikes. Over time both the river and the dikes have come to stand well above the surrounding alluvial plain.

and because the alluvial plain was virtually bereft of rocks, another ingredient was needed to strengthen the protective works and to repair breaches of the dikes during floods. The solution, such as it was, lay in a remarkable plant called kaoliang.

Kaoliang is a grain sorghum with a variety of virtues beyond its use as a food for both humans and animals. It is employed in roofing houses and in providing temporary shelters on the plain. When dried it makes fuel, a commodity in critically short supply on the largely treeless plain.

By far the greatest value of kaoliang, however, rests in its extensive root system, which traps and holds large amounts of silt, and thus forms a formidable barrier to river water. For more than 2,000 years, kaoliang stalks have been stripped of their kernels and leaves, then bound by hemp ropes into bundles that are placed with the roots toward the river, so as to provide facing for the silt dikes. And enormous bales of kaoliang are assembled to plug breaks in the vulnerable dikes after a flood.

The method works well enough—for a time. The great drawback is that kaoliang rots after about two and a half years of exposure to water. When it does, new bundles are piled on top of the old ones, and by their weight the bundles force the decaying matter into the mud of the river's bed. The facing of the levee thus rests on a rotten foundation and is increasingly vulnerable to the scouring action of the river. As the water erodes away the rotten underpinnings of the levee, the entire barrier may collapse—and life on the Great Plain is menaced.

In 1926 an American named Walter Lowdermilk, a soil conservationist who had been called in as a consultant to the Chinese government, reflected on the stoic courage of the farmers in the face of their implacable enemy. The Yellow River dikes, he wrote, had been built "by the hand labor of millions of men—without machines or engines, without steel or timber. These millions of farmers with bare hands have built, through thousands of years, a stupendous monument to human cooperation and the will to survive. I meditated on what these Chinese farmers had endured, toiling on in a situation that was hopeless. For

The 2,878-mile-long Yellow River winds a horseshoe-shaped course from the highlands of central China to the Gulf of Chihli, a northern arm of the Yellow Sea. Twice along its sinuous path, the Yellow passes through a region in northern China known as the loess plateau *(purple),* where it picks up enormous quantities of thick, yellow silt blown eastward in eons past from the Gobi Desert.

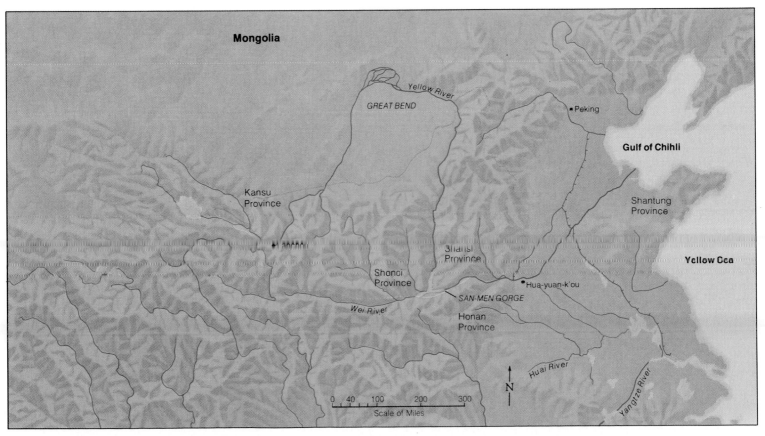

there was no end to the demand of the river for higher and higher dikes. As it annually dropped its burden of silt, it lessened the capacity of the channel between the dikes to carry flood waters."

Despite all efforts to build and maintain the dikes, the Chinese have learned to expect breaches in the levees two years out of three and major breaks, with calamitous floods, practically every other year. There were two major breaches in 1921 and a dismaying four in 1929. There have been a few good periods as well, but the river is never kept in total check for very long. The average expanse covered by an inundation is 3,200 square miles, though the greatest floods can swamp about three times that area.

During a major flood, the churning, silt-laden water may literally tear the defenses apart. Miles of dike can be swept away in a few hours, and billions of tons of water cascade onto the alluvial plain. Fanning out as an advancing lake, the flood seeks a new route to the sea, depositing a thick carpet of sediment as it goes. In most instances, the breach is closed within a relatively short period of time; the lake evaporates or drains away, revealing a wasteland. The riverbed below the breach by now is also dry and represents a second disaster. When the flow is diverted from the original channel, the speed of the water in the bed below the breach drops dramatically—and as it slows, vast quantities of silt, now too heavy for the sluggish stream to carry, are deposited on the bed. One of the greatest problems for Chinese engineers struggling to return the Yellow River to its former channel after a catastrophic flood has been the choking up of the bed below the breach as the remaining water in the channel gradually drains to the sea.

But in the greatest floods all of this is academic, for the escaped river often cannot be contained for months, and even years; eventually it finds a new route to the sea: the channel of another river, one of its own earlier channels or an entirely new channel carved during the flood.

In the last 3,500 years, there have been 26 significant changes in the Yellow River's course. Between 602 B.C.—the year of the first recorded course change—and 1288, the river emptied into the sea between Tientsin and the Shantung peninsula, although in some floods the stream split into two channels, one on each side of the peninsula. Throughout those 19 centuries, the location of its mouth varied by only about 100 miles. Then in 1288, a great flood sent the Yellow charging across country. First it emptied into the Huai, nearly 200 miles to the southeast, then carved a channel across to the Yangtze and wound up emptying into the East China Sea almost 600 miles south of its original position.

During the next 567 years—a period of improvement in civil engineering and of more or less stable government—the Chinese managed to keep a relatively tight rein on their wild river. But in 1855, the Yellow tore open the dike on its left bank at Tungwa Hsiang, about 30 miles east of Kaifeng. During the next six years, while engineers tried repeatedly to repair the shattered dikes, the uncontrolled river wandered northeastward to the sea in many channels. Finally, in 1861, the river settled into its present channel about 500 miles to the north of its 1288 course, emptying into the Po Sea instead of the Yellow Sea.

Since then the Yellow River has temporarily deviated from this channel only twice—and its first shift was the consequence of a catastrophe beyond comprehension.

Communications in 19th Century China were primitive at best, and floods are perhaps the most disruptive of all natural events. The hinterland reports reaching such English-language newspapers as the *North China Herald* were therefore weeks, and even months, behind the actual happenings. Still, since Chinese records were highly colored by government officials who stood to be blamed for

China's kaoliang plant, a member of the grain sorghum family, is proof of the aphorism that there is a use for everything in nature. The kernels are widely consumed as food by man and beast, and the stalk when dried makes an acceptable fuel. But the thick clump of fibrous roots, so seemingly useless, is perhaps the most important part of the plant: When bound together in bundles and used as facing for flood-control dikes, the complex, water-resistant root system captures vast amounts of silt and thus forms an excellent seal against erosion.

An army of peasants labors to contain the floodwaters of the Yellow River in this highly detailed silk painting from the 17th Century. At rear, mallet-wielding workers drive a row of reinforcing wooden pilings into the endangered dike. Their fellows in the foreground gather and bind willow branches into bundles to be packed behind the pilings. Still others dig and haul earth in wicker baskets for use as sealer between the willow bundles.

The strategies the Chinese devise to combat the Yellow River are often quite sophisticated (pages 54-63), but the tools at their command have until recently been the simplest imaginable: masses of peasant workers employing materials close at hand—earth, stones and the fibers of plants.

Witnessing the fight against a flood on the Yellow in 1888, a correspondent for the English-language *North China Herald* wrote that "the whole territory for hundreds of acres resembles a gigantic nest of ants. Thousands of coolies are carrying and wheeling earth. The army of workmen lives in huts and an extemporized city has sprung up to last as long as the work goes on."

For centuries the standard labor quota required each worker to transport and emplace on the dike 1.3 cubic yards of fill per day. And the Chinese exhibited a genius for getting the most out of the dike builders by appeals to pride and self-interest. Superintendents organized competitions with prizes of meat and wine, boots and hats. When the job was nearing completion, the various groups set up large lanterns of red silk as an offering to local gods for their benevolent help, and upon the lanterns were inscribed the names of competition winners. The contests were called "wrestling for the red."

In such fashion, through the ages, millions upon millions of peasants were rallied to the dikes. Today the People's Republic has gone to great lengths to bring modern technology to bear; control dams span the river and earth-moving machines do the daily work of 1,000 men in less than an hour.

But strong backs and willing hands remain crucial to flood control. On a single project in 1955, some 180,000 workers moved 32 million cubic yards of earth and 360,000 cubic yards of stone. And during a period of severe danger along the lower Yellow in 1958, more than one million workers were stationed, 500 to 800 to the mile, with 1,000 or more at key points, along the entire length of a 1,120-mile dike to signal any slight weakening.

Building dikes the traditional way on the Yellow River, Chinese peasants using wooden paddles pound huge bales of kaoliang roots into a firm facing for the levee. The kaoliang was first bound in small, manageable bundles and hauled to the construction site by porters; the bundles were then lashed together with hemp ropes to form enormous bales measuring 49 feet wide and 33 feet long, which were emplaced on the dikes.

Employing a centuries-old technique in dike construction, workers raise tiers of 50-foot-long stone-filled gabions (nicknamed sausages) to a height of 30 feet along the Yellow River. The stones—each small enough to be handled by a single workman—are encased in willow boughs secured by hemp ropes and, when available, steel wires.

Among the first machines to appear on the Yellow River were these heavy tractors employed to pack earth along dikes in the 1950s. However, as the photograph bears witness, the levee builders still depended on hordes of laborers, some with their small, unsteady wheelbarrows, to transport the earth to delivery points marked by red flags.

permitting the Yellow to escape its channel, the English-language papers remain as the only reliable sources for any account of the horror that afflicted the Great Plain beginning in the fall of 1887.

One of the first hints of impending calamity came from a *Herald* correspondent in the Shantung Province city of Tsinan; he reported on September 10 that heavy rains had been falling and the Yellow River was stirring. The rains continued off and on through September and into the middle of October. On the 27th of the month, this item appeared in the *Herald:* "At the moment of going to press we learn that the Yellow River, which has burst its banks over a very long line, has flooded an immense expanse of country in Honan, Shantung and Chihli, and has even reached Anhwei. The loss of life is enormous; numerous cities, towns and villages have been destroyed."

By then, the flood that would eventually be responsible for at least 900,000 and possibly as many as 2.5 million deaths by drowning and starvation and disease had for more than a month been roiling across the North China Plain. The *Herald* was able to piece together reports of the disaster from correspondents in cities in or near the stricken area. A fatal breach had occurred at a sharp bend of the Yellow near the Honan city of Chengchou, 35 miles upstream from Kaifeng and near the site of the 1855 break. There a neglectful government viceroy had allowed the dikes to fall into disrepair. Worse, when warned that the Yellow was rising ominously, he had refused to take emergency maintenance measures because his almanac had told him the time was unpropitious.

On the evening of September 28, 1887, the alarm was sounded and the citizens of Chengchou hurried to man the dike on the Yellow's south bank. The first arrivals found that water was rushing through a gap already 300 feet wide and growing wider with stunning speed. All hope of repairing the dike was gone before the work could even begin. In minutes the breach opened to a width of more than half a mile, and people started fleeing frantically upstream, hoping to stay ahead of the growing torrent. Below the breach, the channel was emptied of water, leaving big junks stranded in mud. The Yellow River was loose on the Great Plain.

Surging generally toward the east, the floodwaters pounded against the walls of Chung-Mow Hsien, a town 10 miles from the river. As the *Herald* somewhat laconically reported, "The unfortunate town is buried with its inhabitants beneath a lake several yards in depth."

Still fed by the water streaming through the breach at Chengchou, the flood surged through at least 1,500 towns and villages and, by the estimate of an American civil engineer who later visited the stricken areas, formed "a lake having a superficial area of that of Lake Ontario"—approximately 10,000 square miles. Such was the extent of the disaster in Honan Province, reported the *Peking Gazette,* that "the Empress Mother has been robbed by it of both sleep and appetite."

By late November, eyewitness accounts had finally begun to reach the *Herald.* "Every night," wrote a correspondent from Anhwei Province, "the sound of the winds and waters, and the weeping and crying, and cries for help, make a scene of unspeakable and cruel distress." Relief efforts had been under way, and the correspondent reported the difficulties encountered by rescuers in small boats: "It is slow work going from terrace to terrace against often both wind and tide; on these terraces from a dozen to 100 families were often congregated. Of houses, not more than one or two in 10 are left with walls in ruins and half under water. Men rest on tops of these houses, and those of the old who do not die of hunger, do of cold."

The *Herald's* reporter went on to describe how people clung desperately to floating straw ricks, "which in a high wind are driven along the water, each with its weeping load of men and women. The tops of poplars which lined the roads now float like weeds on the water, but here and there an old tree with

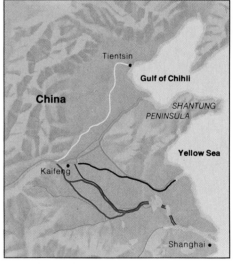

—— 602 B.C. to 1194 A.D.
—— 1194 to 1288
—— 1288 to 1324
—— 1324 to 1855
—— 1855 to 1887, 1889 to 1938, and 1947 to the present
—— 1887 to 1889, and 1938 to 1947

The spectacular shifts of the Yellow River over the last 2,500 years as it has wound its erratic way back and forth across the Shantung peninsula are shown in the color-coded map above. The extent of these course changes caused by floods is unique among the world's great rivers: They range over a distance of 600 miles, from the Gulf of Chihli to the Yellow Sea.

A peasant's cottage lies buried in eight feet of packed alluvial silt on the Yellow River flood plain after the double disaster of flood and drought in 1938. The calamity is thought to have brought death, in one form or another, to 12.5 million Chinese.

thick strong branches has strong men clinging to it crying for help. In one place a dead child floated to shore on the top of a chest where it had been placed for safety by its parents, with food and name attached. In another place a family, all dead, were found with the child placed on the highest spot on a couch, well covered with clothes."

According to its established pattern, the shallow flood lake of the diverted Yellow eventually split into numerous channels. As it had done in 1288, the main channel encroached first on the Huai River and then on the lower Yangtze, far to the south. A Kaifeng observer described the physical desolation left by the flood. "Where the waters of the present flood have subsided," he wrote, "the sand can be seen overspreading the country in a layer from six to ten feet deep, up to the forks of large willow trees." The abandoned bed of the Yellow, he concluded, looked like "one vast Sahara, unrelieved by any oasis."

In the spring and early summer of 1887, drought had caused failure of the area's wheat crop, on which all North China depended. By September, however, heavy summer rains had offered the peasants of the Great Plain the prospect of a good autumn harvest. The flood had shattered such hopes: Millet and beans were drowned, potatoes rotted under silt, even the hardy kaoliang was destroyed. Now famine invaded the land.

Foreign missionaries did their earnest but meager best to relieve the suffering of the refugees who had been uprooted from their tiny tracts of farmland. From Honan, Dr. Thomas Paton of the British and Foreign Bible Society wrote: "There they sit, stunned, hungry, stupid and dejected, without a rag to wear or a morsel of food. Bread, bread is the cry of thousands. The benevolent go in boats and throw bread among the masses here and there. I plead for the perishing multitudes."

On January 6, 1888, the *North China Herald* advised, in a roundabout way, that the gigantic job of plugging the Chengchou breach had begun. "Mssrs. Frazar & Co. sold an Edison's Incandescent Light to the Chinese authorities," reported the newspaper, explaining that this enabled dike repair work to continue at night.

After many centuries of practice, Chinese engineers were perhaps the world's most adept at the massive chore of mending a dike that had been torn asunder by torrential waters. Still, the task could only be long and dangerous; thousands of tons of earth had to be moved in wheelbarrows and passed from hand to hand in buckets; stones were transported for 100 or more miles in small, two-wheeled mule- or ox-drawn carts; the thousands of feet of damaged dike were subject to constant crumbling and, when wet, the silt facing was so slippery that workers went sliding to their death in the river below.

In October 1888, more than a year after the Yellow had broken through, a *Herald* correspondent visited the site of the breach, which had been narrowed to less than 150 yards. From the top of the dike, said the reporter, "we look down some 40 feet on the river below, which pours through a strait about 400 feet wide, with a current of eight or nine miles an hour, in a stream 100 feet deep. Huge whirlpools in the centre of the gap show the immense force of the volume of water." And the correspondent continued, "What now are the materials with which it is proposed to force this body of water, much against its will, into its channel? They are five: sticks, stones, stalks, sand, and bricks."

For the most part, silt and the usual kaoliang facing had been used to build up the broken dike and narrow the gap. Now, with the end in tantalizing sight, came the formidable challenge of closing the last few hundred feet, through which the river rushed with frustrated fury under six-foot waves. Sausage-shaped containers were fashioned from willow branches, filled with stones and then rolled into the breach. To close the final few feet, a kaoliang plug was lowered into the gap and hundreds of workers with baskets of earth and stones swarmed in to complete the seal.

It was early in 1889 before the great breach of the Yellow River was at last closed. By then, pestilence had added its afflictions to flood and famine, and an estimated half million people died of cholera. But the Yellow was back in its course, where it remained until diverted once again—by a reckless and desperate act.

There was certainly ample precedent for the deed. In ancient times, during the period of the Warring States, from 404 to 221 B.C., when warlord fought warlord without respite, the Yellow was employed as a weapon of combat, and the dikes were often deliberately cut in rainy seasons to flood enemy territory. In 923 A.D. the tactic was revived by a Liang Dynasty general named Tuan Ning, who ruptured a levee while at war against the Later T'ang Dynasty; though 1,000 square miles of land was ravaged, the T'ang warriors succeeded in routing the Liang. And in 1642, when Li Tzu-cheng, leading a peasant revolt against the dying Ming Dynasty, besieged Kaifeng, he broke the dikes and turned the river against the city. Victory was his, but at an awful cost; of the district's one million people, most of whom had fled to Kaifeng to escape the fighting, no fewer than 900,000 perished in the deluge.

The notion of blasting open the dike must therefore have seemed like the only recourse to the Kuomintang general who on June 6, 1938, was confronted by Japanese troops preparing to advance from near Kaifeng against the key railroad junction of Chengchou, a few miles south of the Yellow. Taking position between Kaifeng and Chengchou at the village of Hua-yuan-k'ou, less than 10 miles west of the 1887 breach, the general ordered his troops on June 9 to break down the south main dike of the river.

The result was beyond his darkest imagining. Far from merely creating a local flood that would stop the Japanese—as it assuredly did—the breach sent the entire bulk of the Yellow River pouring to the southeast. The deluge covered more than 9,000 square miles, drowning an estimated 500,000 Chinese and leaving six million homeless. The embarrassed Kuomintang at first blamed the breaching of the dikes on heavy Japanese artillery, but Kuomintang leader Chiang Kai-shek later confessed that his troops had been responsible—but at the suggestion and under the direction of Soviet military advisers. The plain remained flooded for seven years; when Japan surrendered, two million acres of fertile farmland were still waterlogged.

In 1947, with the help of the United Nations and an American engineer named Oliver J. Todd, the Chinese finally returned the Yellow to its former channel. The restoration was one of the final successes of Chiang's regime. Within three years, the Chinese Communists had won control of the mainland—and with it had inherited the problems of the Yellow River.

On October 30, 1952, Mao Tse-tung, leader of what was now known as the People's Republic of China, climbed to the top of a Yellow River dike and proclaimed, in words that were immediately turned into a slogan for millions of Chinese to live by: "Work on the Yellow River must be done well!"
Chairman Mao's inspirational rhetoric notwithstanding, the Yellow River, as in millennia past, continued to be China's Sorrow during his lifetime. Shortly after coming to power the new People's Republic embarked on a massive, multifaceted flood-control program to repair the ravages of a decade of wartime neglect. China's new rulers announced that they would combine new ways with old; they called it "walking on two legs." On the lower reaches of the Yellow River, work on the dikes resumed with a vengeance; each winter and spring 300,000 to 400,000 peasants were called upon to trundle their wheelbarrows in the never-ending task of building, repairing—and, of course, heightening—the levees.

The Chinese rebuilt and improved a total of 1,100 miles of dikes. They

Sitting high and dry on a rocky ledge far above the Yangtze River in China's hinterland, a shallow-draft steamer is the victim of a receding flood. During its monumental floods, the Yangtze, second only to the Yellow in death and destruction, at times rises more than 100 feet above its normal stage.

To the Chinese, the Yangtze is known as the Long River. It rises in the Himalayan plateau and descends through one of the world's most populous regions until it finally debouches into the East China Sea after a course of 3,400 miles. Though not so heavy with silt or as flood prone as its northern sister, the Yellow River, the Yangtze has averaged a major deluge every 10 years.

Usually the Yangtze discharges 5.76 million gallons of water per second into the sea. But in times of flood the volume can double and the river often breaks out onto a 70,000-square-mile plain along its middle and lower reaches. That area comprises only 1.5 per cent of China's land mass, but it is home to 230 million people who produce 45 per cent of the nation's rice and other grains. When the Yangtze bursts its banks, the magnitude of disaster strains the imagination.

In 1931, after weeks of unremitting rain, the Yangtze crested 97 feet above its normal stage. More than 3.7 million Chinese died, mainly from famine—and property losses were reckoned at $1.4 billion in American dollars, an astronomical sum for the day.

But the Chinese have always fought back valiantly. When the Yangtze flooded again in 1954, three million peasants and soldiers mobilized to strengthen dikes and repair earthen dams. When the river broke through defenses near the city of Wuhan in Hopeh Province, Peking Radio reported that 10,000 peasants with straw mats on their backs stood waist-deep in the water to form a human dike until their places could be filled with sandbags.

The Chinese were unwavering in their drive to recover from the 1954 deluge. "Where the flood recedes an inch, we replant an inch," exhorted one government slogan. Even so, 30,000 people perished—again, mostly from hunger.

As on the Yellow, the People's Republic of China has made Yangtze flood control a top priority. In the quarter century following the 1954 calamity, the government fortified or built 20,000 miles of dikes and enlarged flood storage capacity by creating huge detention reservoirs capable of holding 41 million acre-feet of water. (An acre-foot equals one acre covered to a depth of one foot.) In 1981, when the river again rose more than 90 feet above normal, the floods were so well contained that fewer than 1,000 people died.

concentrated on one principal line of defense, which they called "the great wall along the river"—850 miles of almost continuous dikes from near Cheng-chou to the sea.

The great undertaking was some years in coming to fruition, and in the summer of 1958, the swollen Yellow presented its direst threat since the war. Heavy rainfall on three tributaries that joined the river from the west near San-men Gorge brought one of the highest flood crests of the century to the Yellow. Once again the Chinese mobilized against their mortal enemy. Wrote a Chinese author in an account that, despite its propagandistic overtones, bespoke truly desperate moments: "A million people headed by Party and government leaders rushed to fight the flood. 'As long as we are here, the dikes will stand firm!' they declared heroically. 'If the water rises, the dikes will rise still higher!' "

Just how much damage was inflicted by this flood remains in question. One Chinese authority on the Yellow states that the dikes were breached in five places, but that only relatively minor damage ensued. Other Chinese reports claim that the rising waters came to within inches of the tops of the dikes but did not breach them. At any rate, when the rains abated and the flood receded the cadre of flood fighters had won a narrow yet signal victory.

Dike maintenance continued to be a way of life on the North China Plain— but with greater success and more visible results than before. Rows and rows of willows were planted along the dikes to strengthen them; stone revetments were laid to further fortify the levees; stone spur dikes were constructed at sharp angles into the river to reduce the rate of flow and thus erosion at vulnerable spots along the main dikes. Cottages at intervals along the dikes housed dike watchers, members of communes charged with basic duties of dike upkeep, such as ensuring that there were adequate supplies of ready repair materials for the flood season.

But Chinese planners recognized the need for other flood-control strategies to supplement the dikes. Amid waves of optimism, Chinese leaders unveiled their master scheme for taming the Yellow once and for all. "This Yellow River plan" cried Vice Premier Teng Tse-hui at the National People's Congress in 1955, "is something grand."

It was indeed—the most ambitious river-management project yet launched by the People's Republic. The goal was to prevent silt from reaching the lower reaches of the river. No fewer than 46 new dams were to be arrayed in staircase form throughout the length of the river, from the Chinghai uplands west of Lanchou to near Tsinan on the lower alluvial plain. Some 25 dams sited in a series of gorges in the loessland along the east side of the Great Bend were to trap the Yellow's silt before it reached the North China Plain. Central to the scheme was to be a huge edifice at San-men Gorge, where the Yellow is briefly split by two rocky islands into three channels known variously as the Gate of Gods, the Gate of Man and the Gate of Ghosts. The San-men Gorge Dam was to stand nearly 400 feet high and span more than 3,000 feet, and its reservoir, encompassing 1,200 square miles, would hold about 29 million acre-feet of water—and silt.

To be sure, the reservoir would last only about 50 years before sediment rendered it useless. But the planners reasoned that half a century would give ample time for an enormous soil conservation program to come into effect. The conservation plan called for sweeping agricultural improvements, such as terracing 4.5 million acres of land on steep slopes and irrigating about one million acres of farmland. Moreover, it included planting up to one billion trees— pine, willow and poplar, and orchards of apples, pears and peaches—on more than 3.5 million acres of the loess plateau to stabilize the soil and prevent it from eroding into the streams that led to the Yellow River. The trees would bring other benefits as well: fruit to eat, wood for fuel and lumber for building.

Following the Revolutionary dictum to turn "low hills and gentle slopes into terraced fields, gullies into orchards," farmers transformed the landscape along the Yellow River in Shensi Province. The contour terracing has an important flood-control effect: It impounds rain water on the hillsides and prevents the erosion of soil into the already silt-heavy river.

"In 12 years," the Minister of Forestry confidently proclaimed in 1956, "China will be a green land."

Unfortunately, the plan posed one problem after another. Construction of the San-men Gorge Dam was begun in April 1957, with Soviet advisers working from Soviet designs. Early in 1960, after the great schism between the Union of Soviet Socialist Republics and the People's Republic of China, the Russians packed their bags and went home—taking with them their San-men blueprints. Nonetheless, the Chinese finished the job soon afterward—only to discover to their horror that their erstwhile allies had miscalculated. The design had been based on an estimate of 1.4 billion tons of sediment to be received annually by the San-men reservoir. Instead, the Yellow was carrying more than

1.6 billion tons into the reservoir. During the first four years of operation, a 60-foot mound of silt piled up against the dam wall.

Trying to make the best of a botched job, the Chinese dug tunnels on the left bank of the reservoir and began sluicing sediment around the dam. The rate of sedimentary accretion in the reservoir slowed, although by 1978—only 18 years after the dam was finished—39 per cent of the designed sediment capacity had been used up. The basin's working life will, therefore, fall somewhat short of the half century originally planned. Whatever benefits the diversion tunnels conferred on the reservoir were canceled by the additional burden of sluiced silt rejoining the stream below the dam. The downstream riverbed build-up, which had dramatically decreased, now began again at an alarming pace. Moreover, several penstocks, or conduits, to power-generating turbines were converted to sluiceways, resulting in a reduction of the dam's electrical capacity to 50,000 kilowatts, barely 5 per cent of the original design goal of 1.1 million kilowatts.

Despite all its problems, the San-men Gorge Dam has eased substantially the ever-present threat of floods originating in the loessland and farther up-stream. The danger, however, remains, and the Chinese recognize that such large, costly projects alone will not solve the problem. In an effort to steal a march on the floods, hydrologists, relying on records from more than 500 stream-flow gauging stations and nearly 1,900 rain gauges throughout the river basin, have developed statistical models to help them forecast the magnitude and speed of Yellow River flood crests. Even a day's warning of an approach-

San-men Gorge Dam, China's first major attempt to bring modern technology to bear on the Yellow River, began operations in 1960 in western Honan Province, where the river plunges 3,000 feet from the loess plateau to the low-lying flood plains. A 27-million-acre-foot reservoir, which resulted from dam renovations completed in 1974, is lowered in the winter and autumn dry season in order to provide additional storage capacity in the spring and summer, when the river is swollen with rain.

ing flood can be enough to evacuate thousands of peasants from critical areas of the flood plain.

But forecasting a flood does not solve the problem of what to do with the unwelcome water once it has arrived. The Chinese have, therefore, built extensive flood-detention basins along the river to store the excess. One such reservoir, near Dongping, was formerly a natural overflow basin for the Yellow and its tributary the Wen. After the alarming flood of 1958, enclosing dikes were laid to increase the storage capacity of the reservoir. Now, during a major flood, water can be diverted from the Yellow to the basin, kept there until the flood subsides and then channeled back into the river.

As for the soil conservation program upon which China's long-term hopes had rested, satisfactory progress was made both at irrigating and at terracing the land. But the forestation program was, in its original form, a dismal and frustrating failure. After traveling in the loess plateau in 1964, German author Harry Hamm reported that "vast tracts of dried-up, withered or damaged young trees served to illustrate that over-hasty mass campaigns alone will not do the trick." The Chinese themselves have since acknowledged that inadequate planning and scientific research, hurried execution of the work in the field and unreasonable expectations of early success led to the failure of this ambitious project.

As a stopgap until erosion prevention becomes effective, numerous silt-settling ponds have been located along the lower reaches of the river. Water is siphoned or pumped into the ponds, where the silt immediately falls to the bottom; the clear water is then either used for irrigation or returned to the Yellow, whose channel it scours with new vigor. Thought by some to be even more effective are hundreds of small reservoirs or check dams that have been sited in the Yellow's middle reaches to capture the silt carried by the main tributaries. And in an attempt to augment the river's scouring of its channel, dredging vessels, their whirring pumps dragging the yellow ooze from the bed, ply to and fro in heavily silted locations.

But the prevention of erosion in the middle and upper reaches of the Yellow remains the only viable long-term answer to the silt problem. In 1980, an official of China's Ministry of Water Conservancy admitted: "Soil erosion on the loess plateau is still very serious, and the amount of silt entering the river is becoming larger and larger all the time. This clearly indicates that our strategy and measures in harnessing the Yellow River are still problematical." **Ω**

RECAPTURING A RENEGADE RIVER

When the Yellow River burst from its banks in July 1935, the flooding was unusually severe. The waters inundated 6,000 square miles of the North China Plain, leaving numberless dead and millions homeless. An American engineer named Oliver J. Todd was in the area at the time, and his photographs of the struggle against the Yellow provide a rare glimpse of Chinese flood-control methods in the 1930s.

The major problem was a 1.5-mile breach torn in the levee in the western Shantung Province through which the waters poured at the rate of 3.75 million gallons per second. An army of 35,000 peasants was soon mobilized to repair the levee. Some 15,000 of the workers first constructed four dikes out into the river a short distance above the break in the main levee. The dikes extended to midriver and were placed at an angle diagonal to the flow: Their purpose was to deflect the water racing through the break and to reduce its flow.

At the same time, on the far bank a second group of 20,000 workers commenced excavating a canal around both the levee break and the main channel of the Yellow. It took two months of round-the-clock labor to complete the canal. But it was not put into immediate use—that would come later, at the climactic moment in the struggle.

Meanwhile, the first brigade of flood fighters turned from the diversion dikes to rebuilding the broken levee, working from both ends toward the middle of the breach. After three months, the gap had been reduced to about 130 feet. At this point, the canal on the opposite bank was opened. And it had the desired effect: The river rushed into the canal, swiftly reducing the flow at the almost-repaired levee.

The closing of the final gap took a week. Workers rolled giant bundles of stones and bales of tough kaoliang stalks into the breach, dumped bags of earth and sand on top, then waited several days for silting to close small leaks. Four months after the peasant army took on the river, the new dike held fast, and the river was returned to its bed once again.

Chinese troops, mobilized to help fight the flood, carry bundles of kaoliang stalks for use in repairing a breach in the Yellow River levee in Shantung Province. The Chinese have been battling the river for more than 40 centuries, and estimates of the dead over that period range as high as 10 million.

Using crude wheelbarrows, Chinese workers rush
loads of rock to the riverbank. Since the immediate
area of flood plain was almost devoid of stone, the
Chinese brought their supplies by railroad and
riverboat from quarries as far away as 160 miles.

In an assembly area near the river, workers ready
bundles of willow branches and kaoliang stalks for
transport by boat to the dike break. The willows
have been fashioned into the casings called "sausages,"
which after being filled with rocks will form part
of the foundation of the rebuilt levee.

As the floodwaters continue to eat away at the levee, teams of workers roll a 50-foot-long, stone-filled sausage into the gap. More than 1,000 of these cumbersome bundles were required in order to reconstruct 50 yards of broken dike.

After a gap in a small, secondary dike has been sufficiently narrowed, a rope net is stretched over the breach. Known as a "dragon net," it will be filled with a great bale of kaoliang stalks and other sealing material; a crisscross of hemp ropes braces the walls of the dike while the work is going on.

Piled high with kaoliang, the dragon net is slowly lowered into the gap by workmen who gradually release the ropes that secure the net to stakes on the riverbank. Beneath the plug, the Yellow swirls through the gap at nearly 4,000 gallons per second.

Red tags flutter overhead as an eight-man team operates a 90-pound stone flapper, which tamps down loose soil shoveled onto the top of the dike. The job of heaving aloft and then dropping the flapper required close coordination, and the tags provided visual cues to the men working the ropes, who repeated a rhythmic chant as an aid to precision.

A city of grass-mat tents provides cramped sleeping quarters for the thousands of dike rebuilders, who earned the equivalent of 15 cents a day for their herculean labors. In the foreground, workers shovel dirt into sacks to be trundled by handcart to the river.

Chapter 3

TAMING THE MIGHTY MISSISSIPPI

The first Europeans to lay eyes on the Mississippi River were the tatterdemalion survivors of Hernando De Soto's ill-fated expedition to the New World in 1539. The Spanish adventurers had come in search of gold. But they found only pestilence and death along the banks of the great river. The Spaniards did, however, witness and record an awesome event that had for centuries shaped the lives of the local Indians—and that would profoundly affect future generations of white settlers.

De Soto's men were building boats to take them downriver to the Gulf of Mexico when pelting rains signaled the advent of another North American spring. Soon afterward, wrote an expedition member named Garcilaso de la Vega, "God, our Lord, hindered the work with a mighty flood, which began to come down with an enormous increase of water." The rising torrent "overflowed the wide level ground between the river and the cliffs that loomed some distance away; then, little by little it rose to the top of the cliffs. Soon it began to overflow the meadows in an immense flood."

De la Vega, who had a sharp eye, also noticed something that was perhaps as significant as the flood itself. The Indians, he wrote, "build their houses on the high land, and where there is none, they raise mounds by hand and here they take refuge from the great flood."

From those heaps of earth, erected by an early people to protect themselves from the ravages of the river to whose banks they were irresistibly drawn, has risen the world's most extensive, elaborate and expensive system of flood-control works. In the epic struggle to contain the Mississippi and its tributaries, crude digging tools have long since given way to monster machines that can transform large tracts of the earth's surface in a trice. And with the awful inspiration provided in the 1920s by a single Mississippi flood—which may have been the greatest natural disaster in American history—long-held and falsely based theories of river dynamics underwent revolutionary change.

Nearly a century ago an old paddle-wheel pilot wrote that no matter how much mind and muscle men might pit against the Mississippi, they "cannot tame that lawless stream, cannot curb it or confine it, cannot say to it, Go here or go there, and make it obey."

The writer was Mark Twain, and he was correct—up to a point. The Mississippi still floods, and it always will. Hydrologists shudder at the nightmarish thought that most or all of the river's countless tributaries might someday come into spate at the same time, causing a superflood whose dimensions would defy calculation. Nevertheless, flood-prevention projects on the Mississippi and its tributaries have had demonstrable effects for the better. There is as much rain-

Plumes of steam rise in the still night air over a big paddle-wheeler waiting with its gangplank lowered while a Mississippi flood victim hurriedly packs his belongings aboard two skiffs. A pair of mules and a cow have taken refuge on the front porch of the flooded house in this 19th Century engraving.

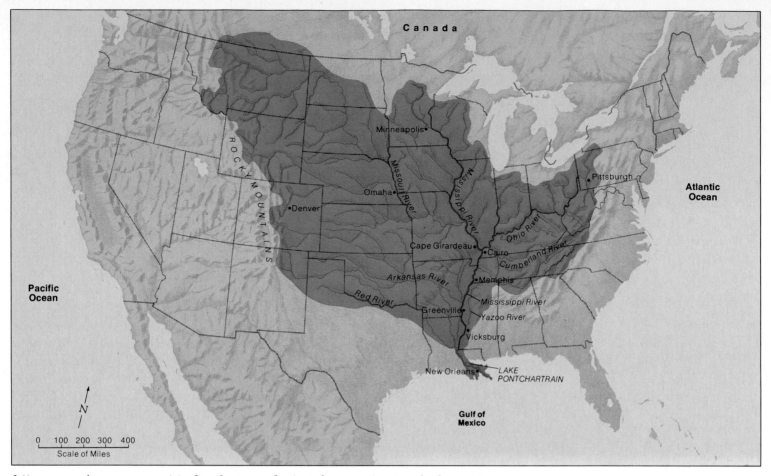

Rill, rivulet, brook, stream and bayou conjoin to form the great river network of the Mississippi, which gathers its water from 31 states and two Canadian provinces. All told, the drainage basin of the Mississippi system covers more than a million square miles, and heavy rainfall in one segment can send a flood crest coursing downriver into areas that may have been dry for weeks.

fall as ever, but catastrophic floods occur far less frequently than before. Moreover, when flooding does take place, the water is so distributed as to diminish the danger to human life and decrease the damage to valuable property.

Such achievements have been wrought on a river system astonishing in its scope and bewildering in its complexity. From a small, shallow lake named Itasca nestled amid the pine forests of northern Minnesota trickles a stream normally no more than a dozen feet wide and 18 inches deep. It is the Mississippi River, just setting forth on its 2,348-mile journey to the Gulf of Mexico near Head of the Passes, 120 miles below New Orleans.

Some 1,300 miles from its source near Cape Girardeau, Missouri, the Mississippi undergoes a dramatic geologic and hydrologic transformation. The upper river, although large and sometimes unruly, is dwarfed in its size and in the magnitude of its floods by the lower Mississippi. Cascading over falls, tumbling down rapids and coursing on a rocky bed between 300-foot bluffs, the upper Mississippi picks up relatively little sediment during much of its descent from the northern uplands. However, at Cape Girardeau the Mississippi enters a majestic alluvial valley, 600 miles long and ranging in width from 30 to 125 miles. Across the almost-level bottom lands of this valley and the vast delta region that lies beyond, the lower Mississippi slowly twists in a tortured sequence of sweeping curves, horseshoe bends and hairpin turns. By the time it reaches the Gulf it carries the waters of perhaps 100,000 streams, many of them insignificant, but some of them ranking among the world's most formidable rivers: the Missouri, Ohio, Arkansas and Red.

The Mississippi's tributary system is a marvel and, to river engineers, a misery. Its drainage basin covers a total area of about 1.25 million square miles in 31 states and two Canadian provinces; it extends westward to within 500 miles of the Pacific Ocean and eastward to within 225 miles of the Atlantic. Only the drainage basins of the Amazon and the Congo are larger. More than

40 of the Mississippi's tributaries are navigable for large parts of their lengths, and it is possible for a vessel of 1,500 tons to make a generally west-east journey of 2,000 miles on the tributaries and main stem of the Mississippi, from Sioux City, Iowa, to East Brady, Pennsylvania.

Above and below the geological break at Cape Girardeau, the Mississippi's hydrological dynamics are radically affected by immense accretions of water from two tributaries, each capable of producing its own ferocious floods.

In its trek across the Great Plains and the central lowlands, the 2,533-mile Missouri, the longest river on the North American continent, annually scours and carries away millions of tons of fertile soil. Three miles below Alton, Illinois, it joins the Mississippi in a wild tide of swirling brown water. Indeed, when the French explorers Jolliet and Marquette encountered the mouth of the Missouri in flood, they reported that in all their travels they had seen "nothing more frightful." Thus, to the comparatively clear waters of the upper Mississippi is added much of the huge sedimentary load that is both bane and blessing to the region below.

The Ohio, which joins the Mississippi at Cairo, Illinois, is even more massive. Into the great river it annually pours almost 60 trillion gallons of water—almost one and a half times the combined flow of the Missouri (17.2 trillion) and the upper Mississippi (23.2 trillion). Formed at Pittsburgh, Pennsylvania, by the junction of the Allegheny and the Monongahela, and fed by such major tributaries as the Wabash, the Cumberland and the Tennessee, the Ohio is one of the world's foremost commercial waterways, annually carrying about 100 million tons of coal, 20 million tons of petroleum products, 10 million tons of chemicals and 50 million tons of other commodities.

However, by climatic misfortune, the entire Ohio basin lies in the path of the cyclonic storms that sweep the continent from southwest to northeast, bringing torrential rains, especially from January through May. "On such occasions," wrote the early-19th Century naturalist John James Audubon, "the

Ohio itself presents a splendid, and at the same time an appalling spectacle; but when its waters mingle with those of the Mississippi, then is the time to view an American flood in all its astonishing magnificence."

From the swift-running upper Arkansas to the sluggish Yazoo and from the Madison, which rises high in the Rocky Mountains, to the Red, which gushes from deep within a Texas ravine, the tributaries of the Mississippi vary vastly. Yet each contributes the weight of its water to the floods of the lower Mississippi. For example, of the estimated 240 billion gallons of water that flowed through the alluvial valley in the flood year of 1927, about 36 per cent came from the Ohio, 13 per cent from the Missouri, 13 per cent from the upper Mississippi, 9 per cent from the Arkansas, 8 per cent from the White, 4 per cent from the Red and 17 per cent from myriad other streams.

As men first laid plans to tame the lower Mississippi it must have been clear that they would have to control its tributaries as well. Yet it was only natural that they should have begun their seemingly endless task in the most obvious place—the lower Mississippi itself.

Le Blond de la Tour, an old soldier and engineer for the French Crown, was dismayed by the directive in 1718 that required him to build a fortified shipping center on the Mississippi River about 120 miles above the Gulf of Mexico. De la Tour protested that the town would forever be subject to inundations from the muddy torrent surging past its doorstep. But his colonial superior, the Sieur de Bienville, had his mind set on the location, both for the fertility of the surrounding land and because the river offered a superb avenue of transportation to the Gulf of Mexico. Bienville brusquely told the engineer to get on with the job.

De la Tour dutifully set to work. He did, however, hedge his bet to the extent of instructing that "a dike or levee be raised in front, more effectually to preserve the city from overflow." By 1727 Nouvelle Orléans—the first permanent European settlement on the Mississippi—spread over 1,280 acres of bottom land bordering the vast river. And guarding it, after a pathetic fashion, was an embankment 5,400 feet long, 18 feet across at its top—and a scant four feet high. In this manner, civilization and attempts at flood control came concurrently to the lower Mississippi.

Within the next century, cotton became king on the Mississippi delta, while the immense valley was transformed into a granary served by cities;that thrived on river commerce. The levees kept pace with the growth of population, and where the river had once sloshed over its banks it was now imprisoned—at least in theory—for long stretches between man-made dirt walls.

The system, however, was at best a patchwork proposition. As in the early days on the Yellow River, owners of riverfront land were interested only in building and maintaining the levees that protected their own property. During periods of high water, downstream planters suffered when their neighbors above were either too lazy or too poor to keep the dikes in good repair.

Improved organization was clearly required, and by the 1830s, levee districts with enforcement powers had begun to form. In Washington County, Mississippi, for example, levee inspectors examined the dikes at least twice a week, and when workers were needed they were authorized to "call out all slaves, men and women, within five miles of the levee." Since rooting swine were a major cause of dike damage, the inspectors were also empowered "to kill hogs running at large within two miles of the levee."

Meanwhile, the federal government in the form of the U.S. Army Corps of Engineers had begun to make its presence felt on the Mississippi. But at first the involvement of the corps was strictly limited: The engineers worked solely to improve the river's channel for navigation; Congress, aware of the large costs of flood control, had not authorized them to enter the battle against floods.

Congress' hand was finally forced by a great inundation in 1849 and by another the following year. Only then did the legislators grant funds for the Corps of Engineers to conduct an extensive study of flood-control possibilities on the lower Mississippi.

To complete that study required more than a decade. The 456-page report was a masterpiece of compiled facts and figures—but its flood-control recommendations were to prove sadly inadequate. Both in its reasoning and in its main conclusion, the report relied heavily on a theory developed by a 17th Century Italian engineer named Domenico Guglielmini. It was Guglielmini's idea that alluvial rivers always transport sediment to the full extent of their carrying capacity, with the speed of the flow being the determining factor. As the speed increases or decreases, so does the carrying capacity. Therefore, he said, if a river's waters were confined between levees, the volume and velocity of the stream would increase, and it would deepen its bed by scouring. The happy result would be less frequent flooding. Conversely, any flood-control methods that diminished volume and velocity—such as storage reservoirs and diversion channels—were bound to be harmful.

Although sound in principle, Guglielmini's theory did not take sufficient account of the complexities of river erosion and sediment transportation over an alluvial bed—especially the relationships between channel shape and capacity, type and size of sedimentary load, and rate and volume of flow. Indeed, under certain circumstances, a swiftly flowing captive stream might simply eat away at its confining banks without significantly deepening its channel. Nevertheless, Guglielmini's theory, as promulgated by the U.S. Army engineers in 1861, was the basis for what became known as the "levees only" policy of flood control on the lower Mississippi. As such, it would persist into the 20th Century, and its effect would be pernicious beyond belief.

Before the policy could be put into effect, the Civil War intervened. Levees fell into disrepair—constantly clawed by the river, riddled by burrowing animals, sundered by trenches in which troops defending the waterway had fought and died. But no sooner did the shooting stop than the massive effort to control the Mississippi got under way with a desperate energy.

Slaves were no longer available, but black laborers continued to work on the levees. They were joined by thousands of European immigrants seeking a new life in America. Paid out of local taxes for each cubic yard of earth that they moved in their wheelbarrows, they transported millions of tons. Yet there was always more work to be done. For one thing, the levees were damaged by crayfish, four-inch crustaceans whose favored abode was inside tunnels they dug into the river-side faces of the dikes. Water penetrated through the crayfish holes making necessary extensive repairs. By so providing the immigrant workers with continued employment, the little crayfish became known along the length of the lower Mississippi as "the Irishman's friend."

By 1880 the entire 700-mile lower Mississippi Valley, from St. Louis to the river's mouth, had been organized into levee districts under the general supervision of the Mississippi River Commission, a seven-member group newly established by Congress. It was required by law that the president and two other members of the commission be officers of the Corps of Engineers—and these men were invariably dedicated to the policy of levees only. Furthermore, because of the federal government's parsimony, most of the cost of building and maintaining the levees had to be borne by local taxpayers.

Even as the levee system expanded, floods on the lower Mississippi continued without letup either in frequency or in fury—at least in part because of the silt that was choking the captive river. In doleful succession, major floods struck the region in 1881, 1882, 1883, 1884, 1886 and 1890; during that decade, water poured through more than 500 crevasses, as breaks in the Mississippi levees were called, and each crevasse provided an occasion of crisis. Year after

South America's Gentle Giant

Even though it pumps 10 times as much water through its silty veins each year as does the Mississippi, South America's Amazon River—the largest watercourse in the world—is a gentle giant when it comes to flood. Two geographical oddities help account for the Amazon's relatively predictable and benign habits.

First, both its major tributaries, the Rio Negro and the Madeira River, draw their source waters from regions that lie on opposite sides of the Equator and have different rainy seasons. Thus they tend to cancel each other out as contributing factors to the Amazon's flood cycle.

The second peculiarity of the Amazon is the series of large, shallow lakes that have formed in the flood plain alongside its main trunk. During floods these lakes act as a kind of natural flood-control system to store the river's excess waters.

To be sure, the Amazon does occasionally flood far beyond expectation. But even then, so few people live along its banks—and those who do have so wisely adapted to the dangers of floods—that little harm is done.

Twisting through dense equatorial jungle on its course to the Atlantic, the Amazon River cleaves the South American continent at its widest part. The Amazon's widely disparate source waters and a series of natural reservoir lakes (*map*) help minimize the danger of flooding along its 4,000-mile course.

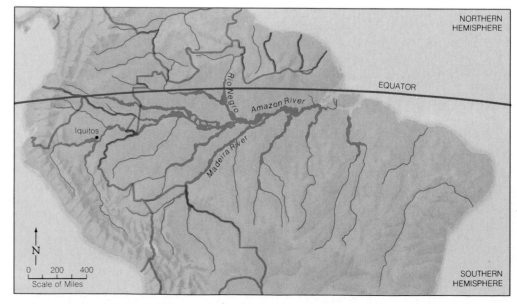

In the Peruvian town of Iquitos, floating cane-and-thatch dwellings ride on logs in the shallows at a bend of the Amazon. Located at the foot of the Andes, this stretch of the river is particularly prone to flood.

year, in day and night shifts, volunteer guards patrolled the levees in fulfillment of an obligation that stood second to none. Said an 1893 appeal for guards in the Greenville, Mississippi, *Democrat:* "To refuse to do your duty proclaims you wanting in those characteristics which prove your patriotism in a time when your country is threatened."

During high-water times, recalled William A. Percy, himself a veteran of guard duty, the "river is a savage clawing thing, right at the top of the levee and sounding at night like the snarl of a beast. It puts ice into your heart when you're trudging the darkness on the slippery berm."

Swinging their lanterns low, the guards looked especially for boils—tiny geysers that spouted at or near the land-side base of the dike. Caused by the pressure of water seeping into the levee through a flawed spot—such as a crayfish or muskrat hole—boils could enlarge themselves with breathtaking speed, setting off a ruinous process of disintegration. "If the geyser runs clear," Percy explained, "it is being filtered and is comparatively harmless; but if it runs muddy, it is in direct contact with the river, and you'd better shoot your pistol, yowl to the next guard, and do something quick."

Standard emergency procedure was to encircle the area with sandbags to the height of the boil. When the sandbag enclosure was filled with water, the pressure was equalized and the boil was no longer a threat. Still, it was a tricky business, and more crevasses were caused by the undermining action of boils than by the river topping the levees.

Entirely aside from sounding the alarm, pistols and shotguns were essential parts of every levee walker's equipment. On each bank of the river, the inhabitants viewed those on the other side with deep suspicion, and dark stories were spread of men in dynamite-laden skiffs crossing the swollen Mississippi so as to blast open breaches in an opposing levee and thereby relieve the pressure on their own dike. In fact, there is no persuasive evidence of any such riverine sabotage. But the guards were guided by the belief, and strangers approached a levee by small boat only at their peril—for the guards also feared that the mere wake of a boat would overtop a levee in time of high water. During one flood, a newsman touring the area reported that his launch had been fired on more than 20 times.

By the turn of the century, immigrant wheelbarrows had mostly given way to more imposing earth-moving equipment, including dump wagons drawn by as many as 16 mules. Except at the mouths of tributaries, the levees now

Flood workers fighting the Mississippi in 1927 attempt to plug a break in a levee at Cairo, Illinois, by pushing a string of boxcars into the breach. A strand of unbroken track still spans the gap even though the railroad bed has been washed away.

stretched for hundreds of miles on both sides of the river between Cairo and the Gulf. The floods, however, continued, with major inundations in 1903, 1912 and 1913, when the height of the flood exceeded all previous records. By then, with burgeoning cities and towns along the river, the damage from a severe flood might reach into the many tens of millions of dollars, astronomical amounts for the time. Under public and political pressure from the beleaguered states of the lower Mississippi, the federal government was inexorably drawn into greater participation in flood control. By act of Congress in 1917, the Mississippi River Commission was authorized to spend $45 million in an arrangement that worked out at a 50-50 division of costs with the local levee districts.

Yet the Corps of Engineers remained adamant in its insistence that levees by themselves could control the Mississippi. Only five years after a major flood in 1922, the Mississippi River Commission proclaimed that the levee system "is now in condition to prevent the disastrous effects of floods."

Even as the commission spoke, forces were gathering that would forever change the nature of flood control on the Mississippi River and its tributaries.

In August 1926, unusually heavy rains began to fall over much of the Mississippi's drainage basin. By September, tributaries in eastern Kansas, northwestern Iowa and parts of Illinois lapped over their banks. Throughout the autumn and winter the rains continued: On New Year's Day, 1927, a Cumberland River gauge showed a record reading of 56.2 feet, more than 41 feet above the reading of the previous August. The great Ohio, which receives the Cumberland's waters, rose ominously to a 44.9-foot reading on the gauge at Cairo; in August of 1926 the gauge had stood at 18.1. The rain slackened in February, but in March the downpours began again, and a roiling tide moved into the valley of the lower Mississippi, its crest advancing at more than 10 miles a day. On April 9, Major Donald Connolly of the Corps of Engineers in Memphis stoutly declared, "We are in condition to hold all the water in sight."

Twelve days later, the Mississippi broke loose.

At Mound Landing, 18 miles above Greenville, the river curved to the east, and the concave levee at that point bore the full brunt of the rushing water. By

Clusters of roofs and treetops stand like islands in a sea during the 1927 Mississippi River flood. Cattle are gathered on points of high ground that are known as Indian mounds because Indian tribes used them as places of refuge during earlier floods.

April 20, the dike had clearly weakened: Telltale jets of water shot up on the land side, and a woman who lived nearby later recalled that the bubbles at the levee were "just boiling, boiling, boiling." People working on the levee could actually feel the embankment trembling beneath their feet as the Mississippi pounded against it.

Throughout the chilly night of April 20, engineers, plantation owners, small farmers and townspeople struggled in a steady rain to save the levee. Among them were the descendants of slaves whose forced labor had originally built the levee; these people were now fighting to save their own homes and patches of land. "In the glare of improvised flares and floodlights they swarmed over the weak spot," wrote the flood veteran William Percy. "But about daylight, while the distraught engineers and labor bosses hurried and consulted and bawled commands, while the 5,000 Negroes with 100-pound sandbags on their shoulders trotted in long converging lines to the threatened point, the river pushed, and the great dike dissolved under their feet."

In Greenville, General Alexander G. Paxton of the Engineers, talking by telephone to one of the Mound Landing flood fighters, had just been told: "We can't hold it much longer." Recalled Paxton: "Then followed three words that I shall remember as long as I live—'There she goes!' "

How many of the hapless workers were swept to their deaths is unknown. The river's waters roared through an enormous breach that swiftly widened to nearly a mile. An engineer later estimated that the volume of water rushing through the gap was as great as that hurtling over Niagara Falls.

As the torrent fanned out over the flat delta, it appeared to one planter as "a tan-colored wall seven feet high, and with a roar as of a mighty wind." Author William Faulkner described the harrowing experience of a convict and a woman the man had rescued. Their skiff "seemed to stand erect on its stern and then shoot scrabbling and scrambling up the curling wall of water like a cat, and

With canvas tents providing some shelter and a makeshift outhouse perched on its bow, a wooden river barge crammed to the gunwales with refugees is nudged along the Sunflower River in western Mississippi during the 1927 flood. More than 650,000 people were rendered homeless by this great inundation of the Mississippi and its tributaries.

soared on above the licking crest itself and hung cradled in the limbs of a tree." Then the little vessel was plucked up again and tumbled along a maelstrom from which "entire trees, the sharp gables of houses, the long mournful heads of mules—rolled up and then down again." Four days later, the woman and the convict were washed up on an Indian mound, battered but still alive.

By the time the flood receded, the water from the Mound Landing crevasse alone would flood more than 2.3 million acres of land. Flowing overland, it swirled around the hills to the east and entered the basin of the Yazoo River, whence it was returned to the main stream of the Mississippi near Vicksburg. The huge accretion of water broke through the levee at Cabin Teele in northeast Louisiana, swamping the area between the Mississippi and the Tensas River.

Across the Mississippi from Mound Landing, the residents of Arkansas City, Arkansas, had witnessed the misfortune of their neighbors with a mixture of sympathy and relief. Wise in the ways of the river, they were confident that the diversion of water through the east-bank Mound Landing breach would diminish the pressure on their own west-side levee.

But their deliverance was short-lived. In the early evening of April 21, a levee burst at Pendleton, Arkansas, 32 miles upstream from Arkansas City, which now lay helplessly in the path of the water as it moved inexorably southward. "You could hear it roaring a long ways off," said Robert Murphy, who lived below Pendleton. "Kind of like, they say, a tornado. Near about that loud." And in Arkansas City, recalled Grady F. Jones, "all the cattle was lowing, all the dogs barking, every rooster crowing, babies crying, women screaming and all hurrying to the high places." Not all. On streets that had been dry at noon, mules still hitched to wagons were drowned by 2 p.m.

Now another danger arose. Whenever a main stream rises higher than a tributary, backwater flows into the subsidiary stream. That is what happened to the Arkansas River, which breached its own levees in a dozen places from its mouth to Little Rock, 100 miles upriver. Near Pine Bluff, 60 miles from the mouth, about 500 people, mostly tenant farmers and their families, fled to a precarious safety on Free Bridge, a mile-long steel span across the Arkansas.

There they were stranded. Floodwaters covered the inclined approaches at both ends of the bridge; a driving wind churned the river and made rescue by boat too perilous to attempt. For three days and nights of cold and rain, the refugees remained on the quivering span. By the time they were finally taken off by boat, two babies had been born on Free Bridge.

By the middle of May, the Mississippi's crest had advanced slowly, irresistibly into the bayou country of Louisiana. Just below the Red River, backwaters from the Mississippi pushed into Bayou des Glaises in the state's cane-growing Sugar Bowl. There, levees had been built to protect such towns as Cottonport, Marksville, Moreauville, Simmesport and Plaucheville. The levee near Cottonport went first, then the others, and within two days the bayou's entire levee system lay ruined.

In angry tide, the floodwaters from Bayou des Glaises and from the Mississippi itself invaded the basin of the swampy Atchafalaya River. Although the massive Atchafalaya levee at Melville had been considered impregnable, it crumbled on May 17. Among those who witnessed the collapse was Turner Catledge, a reporter for the Memphis *Commercial Appeal* and a future managing editor of *The New York Times.* "The water leaped through the crevasse with such fury that it spread into three distinct currents," Catledge reported. "One force shot straight west, wrecking houses, barns and fences as it went." A second current raced due north, quickly eating out 50-foot sections of the Texas & Pacific Railroad embankment, "thus allowing the water to go up into the town proper and completely inundate it. Breakers were shooting through and leaping over each other way up into the streets of the town. A third current struck out from the south. It swept everything before it. Washtubs, work benches, household furniture, chickens and domestic animals were floating away."

On the main stem of the Mississippi, historic New Orleans stood in jeopardy of its very survival. The huge levee protecting the Crescent City—so nicknamed because of the shape of a bend in the river there—would clearly be topped when the flood's crest arrived. The salvation of New Orleans demanded drastic, even pitiless action.

Just below the city, at a place where the Mississippi looped eastward, was the Caernarvon levee. If it were blasted open, topography dictated that the water pouring through the resulting crevasse would drain off to the southeast, taking an overland shortcut through thinly populated St. Bernard and Plaquemines Parishes and emptying into the Gulf at Breton Sound. More important, if the plug was pulled at Caernarvon the level of the water now choking the channel upstream, to New Orleans and beyond, might be lowered.

Protests from the inhabitants of the condemned parishes were of no avail; state authorities sent trucks to convey them and their belongings to refuges in New Orleans. They were promised compensation for their property losses, and National Guardsmen were dispatched to oversee the destruction of the levee.

The first attempt to dynamite the Caernarvon levee was a spectacular failure. The explosive charges—1,500 pounds of dynamite—had been buried on the top of the dike. When they were detonated, the eruption shot tons of earth high into the air—whence it fell straight back down, filling the excavations created by the blast. Only a tiny rivulet escaped through the levee.

A diver, Ted Herbert, volunteered to descend to the bed of the Mississippi to plant charges in the base of the levee. Twice he tried and twice he failed after being so badly buffeted by the swirling current that his diving helmet was twisted askew, almost strangling him. On Herbert's third attempt, the charges were successfully placed—and the levee was soon torn asunder by a tremendous explosion.

Old Man River lies abed with a bad case of the floods in this cartoon from the Philadelphia *Ledger* of May 3, 1927. Secretary of Commerce Herbert Hoover and the commander of the United States Army Corps of Engineers press upon him the age-old remedy for high water—higher levees—while more modern (and, as it turned out, more effective) remedies lie ignored on the bedside table.

As water in vast volume poured through the break, a local official bitterly told newsmen: "You are witnessing the public execution of a parish." Within hours, however, the river gauge just above New Orleans showed that the stage of the flood was falling. The city was saved—and, with the deliberate destruction of the levee at Caernarvon, the notion that levees alone could prevent floods of the Mississippi was forever demolished.

In all its dreadful grandeur, a brown and sullen sea, in places 18 feet deep and 80 miles across, now spread over more than 16.5 million acres in seven states, with Louisiana, Arkansas and Mississippi suffering most. The official death toll was reported at 246, but it may have been as high as 500. Nearly 650,000 people had been driven from their homes. Many thousands were marooned on the levees that still stood. Wrote one survivor, stranded with 50 others on a 20-foot-wide levee past which water was rushing on both sides: "We sit upon the ground in groups, afraid to sleep, too miserable to cry, waiting with forlorn hope for a rescue boat. We have no water except the foul stuff that is all about us. We drink sparingly of it, grimacing, wiping our lips. There is no food. There is no wood. We have no fire."

To avoid a duplication of effort, rescue workers near Greenville nailed strips of red cloth, taken from a flooded dry-goods store, to the roofs of houses as a sign that they were already emptied. Late one evening a boat was passing a home that showed the red emblem. From the place came shrieks and screams. Drawing closer, the boatmen found four panthers crouching terrified in the attic where they had taken refuge.

To the aid of the stricken region came 33,000 rescue and relief workers, almost all of whom were volunteers under the joint direction of Secretary of Commerce Herbert Hoover and the American Red Cross's James Fieser, who because of his long experience in disaster relief was known as Calamity Jim. At their disposal Hoover and Fieser had nearly 6,000 vessels, ranging from 700-ton river steamers to tiny skiffs.

The work could be heartbreaking. In his little launch, powered by a Model-T engine, Herman Caillouet of Metcalfe, Mississippi, saw a house floating by

with a man, a woman and five children on its roof. Recalled Caillouet: "The house was just moving along, you know, and all of a sudden it must of hit a stump or something. And the house flew all to pieces. . . . And you know I never saw a soul come up, not a soul."

Help sometimes came from unexpected sources. The swampy bayous that were part of the river systems in Arkansas had become locally famed as havens for moonshiners who, in dead of night, sped forth in high-powered motor boats to distribute their illegal whiskey along both banks of the Mississippi. Now the bootleggers and their speedy vessels emerged on missions of mercy. Wrote flood historian Percy: "No one had sent for them, no one was paying them, no one had a good word for them—but they came. They scoured the back areas, the forgotten places, across fences, over railroad embankments, through woods and brush, and never rested."

By the time the waters of the lower Mississippi finally receded in July, more than 325,000 refugees had been cared for in 154 Red Cross camps. Officials put the damage at more than $230 million, an enormous figure even in those pre-Depression years of boom and plenty.

For the future of flood control, perhaps the most meaningful statistic of all was that the levees on the lower Mississippi and its tributaries had broken in no fewer than 120 places. As the Chinese had so painfully learned, levees alone were clearly inadequate, and containing the restless river could no longer be treated as primarily a local responsibility. Instead, it was a national obligation—and the critical question was not so much whether the federal government should take over the job, but how.

The U.S. Congress provided its answer in the Flood Control Act of May 15, 1928—a turning point in the history of American efforts to restrain the brute forces that have so frequently drowned the land. During the previous 200 years an estimated total of $292 million in local funds had been spent on lower Mississippi flood works; now, in a single act, the Congress authorized expendi-

Board sidewalks pave "Main Street" of one of the 154 Red Cross Refugee Centers that were set up during the 1927 Mississippi flood. These makeshift cities provided temporary housing for 325,000 flood victims and at the same time served as immunization centers against smallpox and typhoid.

tures of $325 million. While levee expansion and improvement were ordered, so were such measures, hitherto overlooked, as reservoirs and dams on key tributaries. Other elements of the plan included protective coverings to stabilize the natural banks of the river, diversionary floodways to lessen the volume of water in the main stream, an outlet to the Gulf near Berwick, Louisiana, to lower water levels in the Atchafalaya basin, the setting up of a hydraulics laboratory, and emplacement and operation of a system of river gauges. Finally, the Army engineers were now given an almost exclusive franchise for construction of control mechanisms, although responsibility for upkeep of the levees remained with local boards.

To take charge of the flood-control program the newly appointed chief of engineers, General Lytle Brown, turned to an old river hand. Colonel (later Major General) Harley B. Ferguson, his choice as new president of the Mississippi River Commission, described his approach tersely: "The water wants out. We will give it out."

To hasten the Mississippi's water on its way to the Gulf, Ferguson proposed to straighten and shorten its channel with a series of cuts across the necks of meanders. It was a measure he had long advocated—though it was considered heresy by adherents of the levees-only policy.

In its natural wanderings, the Mississippi often looped back on itself to a point where only a few hundred yards remained between the bends of the river. If left alone, the river would eventually break through the neck, creating a natural shortcut; silt would clog both ends of the abandoned loop, leaving an oxbow lake, so called because of its shape, with horns pointing to the river.

Although proposals for artifical cutoffs had long been discussed, they were

In an unlucky development, the levee at Arkansas City, Arkansas, is seen here to have worked in reverse. High water is trapped in the flooded town while the river, at right, is now at a lower level. Red Cross steamers nose into shore bringing supplies to townspeople precariously encamped in the thin line of white tents running down the crest of the levee.

rejected on grounds that the increased velocity of water through the new chutes would make navigation more difficult, and that while upstream stages of the river might be temporarily lowered, the downstream volume of water would be increased. Ferguson disagreed. He argued that the river should be encouraged to rid itself of its choking waters as fast as possible—and that cutoffs were the way to do it.

To excavate a cutoff with a navigable channel was an undertaking of epic proportions. The dredging of a single cutoff in the years 1934 and 1935 required the use of seven enormous dragline machines and the removal of 11.29 million cubic yards of earth. Nevertheless, the engineers persevered and by 1937 they had excavated a fantastic 108 million cubic yards of earth in carving 11 such cutoffs. Along with two that had been allowed to form naturally, these new channels had shortened the river by 115.8 miles in what had been the 331-mile stretch from Rosedale, Mississippi, to Angola, Louisiana, above Baton Rouge. Not only was the river shorter and straighter but, in the business of clearing itself of rising waters, it was considerably more efficient—as would soon be demonstrated.

To preserve the integrity of the new channel and to inhibit further meandering on the old, a mammoth program was launched to protect against erosion of the river's natural banks, from which new levees had in some places been set back by as many as five miles on each side. As water flows against the surface of a bank it exerts pressure against the exposed soil particles, diminishing their cohesion and perhaps dislodging them. The sharper the angle at which the water strikes, the more vulnerable the bank is to erosion.

For almost half a century, revetments to fend off such erosion had been fashioned from cylindrical bundles of willows, tied side by side in units more than half a mile long. But the willow brush became brittle when exposed to the stresses of the river, giving the revetments a life of only eight to 12 years. Following the 1927 flood and after much experimentation, a revetment system was developed that, with remarkably few changes, is still being used.

First, the rough bank was scraped smooth and graded. Then, on specially designed barges, articulated concrete mattresses were assembled in 140-by-25-foot units of reinforced slabs, each four feet long, 14 inches wide and three inches thick. With one end of a unit securely anchored to the riverbank, the barge was backed away, paying the mattress down its ways as it went. The process was repeated until the bank was covered from above the water line to the deepest part of the river's bed. Finally, the upper bank was paved with stone riprap to protect it during floods.

The decades when the levees were built by the local districts had been marked by a lack of uniformity. Some of the ramparts were high and steep; some were squat and gently sloped; some had been carefully engineered; others were little more than rude heaps of earth. Under Ferguson's aegis, standard specifications were set. Levees should be constructed to a height one foot above that of the "maximum possible flood" as defined by the National Weather Service. The Weather Service used the greatest flood of the Ohio combined with the highest levels of the Mississippi, Cumberland and Tennessee Rivers to arrive at the correct figure: The barriers were built 28 feet high, with bases about 10 times as wide as the height.

For the first time, local soil composition was taken into account. If, for example, a levee was made of solidly compacted loam—as was the case about 90 per cent of the time—a 10-foot crown was required, with a slope of 1 foot in every 3.5 feet on the river side and a ratio of 1 in 6.5 on the land side. But if highly permeable and unstable sand made up 75 per cent or more of the levee material, a 12-foot crown was specified, with slopes of 1 in 5 on the river side and 1 in 8 on the land side.

To tackle the prodigious chore of renovating hundreds of miles of substan-

A 1,600-ton barge, at right, slowly backs off from shore, laying a huge mattress of chain-plate concrete on the riverbank and out into the river. Often running for miles along the erosion-prone Mississippi, such revetments prevent the river from changing its course and cutting into fertile farmland or, worse yet, leaving port towns high and dry.

dard levees, bigger and better earth-moving equipment was needed. Draglines mounted on barges with booms up to 165 feet long now engorged as much as 15.5 tons of dirt in a single swallow. Tower excavators, less mobile but able to scoop up and transport even more earth for distances of up to 1,000 feet, spewed as much as 4,000 cubic feet per hour onto the growing levees. By 1937, some 600 miles of main-stream levees had been brought up to standard.

The jewels of the new system—and the very antithesis of the old—were the waterways that, far from holding the river within a line of levees, were constructed so that, under controlled conditions, it might escape, thereby lowering the main stream.

On the Missouri side of the Mississippi River opposite Cairo, Illinois, the federal government purchased flowage rights through a 131,000-acre strip of land that extended 30 miles from Bird's Point to New Madrid. Along the river side of that tract, the old levee was rebuilt with two devices called fuse plugs—sections that were lower than the rest of the barrier, and over which water would flow when the river's overall depth reached 55 feet, comfortably below the 60 feet at which the flood wall protecting Cairo would be topped. During severe floods these plug areas could be lowered still more by removal of their uppermost layers.

In order to contain the flow that came over the upriver fuse plug and into the floodway, another levee was built as far as 10 miles back from the riverfront. By the time the water from the floodway reentered the river through the downriver fuse plug at New Madrid, the threat to the city of Cairo would presumably be relieved.

Considerably more intricate works were built to safeguard New Orleans. The Bonnet Carré Spillway, completed in 1932, was controlled by a 7,000-foot concrete structure set into the riverfront levee on the Mississippi's east bank, about 30 miles upstream from New Orleans. The edifice had 350 bays, each 20 feet wide, in which wooden gates could be individually moved up or down by mobile cranes. If all the gates were raised, up to two million gallons of water per second would pass through into a 5.7-mile floodway, enclosed on each side by guide levees, that led into Lake Pontchartrain and from there to the Gulf of Mexico.

Early in 1937 the entire new system faced its first severe test—in the form of a flood that in some places brought even higher river levels than the inundation of 1927.

The fearful flood of 1937 found its genesis in the torrential rains that, during 25 January days of unremitting storm, dumped an estimated 15 trillion gallons of water on the basin of the Ohio River. From its farthest reach in West Virginia to its mouth at Cairo, the Ohio rose relentlessly, swamping its own banks and emptying into the Mississippi a tide of water without precedent in the turbulent history of that stream.

Cairo, behind its flood wall on a low, narrow neck of land, was imperiled as the river ascended beyond 55 feet; the crest was predicted at 63 feet. At that point, Corps engineers decided to lower the fuse-plug sections of the west-bank levee by removing its top three feet. Foul weather and insufficient time made this impossible. And so, to permit water to pass over the fuse plug, the engineers on January 25 set off dynamite charges that blasted three separate crevasses in the plug. The effect was almost immediate: An estimated one fourth of the Mississippi's flow was diverted into the Bird's Point-New Madrid Floodway, and by that afternoon the flood stage at Cairo had begun to fall; it had reached a peak of 58.6 feet.

Downstream, thousands of workers manned the levees. Said Colonel Eugene Reybold of the Corps of Engineers: "We have organized our main stem levees as in battle. Flood fighters hold each sector of the river, just as we would assign companies, battalions, brigades and divisions in wartime. Each sector commander must maintain at all costs the integrity of his levee line." And although the river reached record heights from below Cairo to the mouth of the Arkansas, not a single main-line levee broke.

Nonetheless, the river remained a mighty force, and it soon became apparent that it would overtop its levees at New Orleans. This time, however, there was no need to send the flood's waters swirling onto the private lands of the people who lived below the city as had been done in 1927. One by one, the gates of the Bonnet Carré Spillway were opened until 285 of the 350 stood agape. By the time the flood crest had passed New Orleans, sufficient water had been diverted into Lake Pontchartrain to cover 1.25 million acres to a depth of 10 feet. And the river's level had been lowered for a stretch of 100 miles.

The havoc wrought by the 1937 flood was colossal—137 dead, about 13,000 homes destroyed, more than eight million acres under water. But the 1927 figures had been much worse. Most of the damage this time had been done either on the Ohio or by the Mississippi's waters backing into other tributaries—which clearly required that more attention be paid to them.

Work on the Mississippi has continued at a steady, grinding pace. By 1945, three more cutoffs had shortened the river by another 36 miles to a total of 176 miles (alas, the river, in its ceaseless, meandering struggle to find its own course, managed to extend its length by 56 miles in the next 15 years). The

Despite its name, Louisiana's Old River is in reality a very young stream. It was created almost by accident less than 200 years ago. Yet today, an uncontrollable flood of this infant among rivers could threaten the welfare of every town along the Mississippi River south of Baton Rouge, including the great Gulf port of New Orleans. How so perilous a situation came about—and what is being done about it—is a complex story involving a total of four rivers, three dams, two canals and a log jam 30 miles long.

In the early 1800s, the Mississippi—to the vast annoyance of riverboatmen—made one of its broadest meanders to the west 80 miles above Baton Rouge at a point known as Turnbull's Bend. This particular bend was also notable as the place where the Red River flowed into the Mississippi and where the Atchafalaya, a small branch choked to a trickle by a prehistoric log jam, set off on its feeble way to the Gulf of Mexico *(top left)*.

In 1831, Henry Shreve, riverboat captain and founder of the city of Shreveport, ordered a channel to be dug across Turnbull's Bend, short-circuiting the river at that point and cutting off the confluences with the Mississippi of the Red and Atchafalaya. The channel was dug and the great river readily accepted the new shortcut, but to everyone's surprise, Turnbull's Bend refused to die. Only the top section of the bend dried up. The lower loop continued to flow, forming a short seven-mile waterway connecting the Mississippi and the two smaller rivers. This vestigial connection became known as Old River.

Then in 1839, the state of Louisiana made a fateful decision to begin burning, blasting and dredging the log jam on the Atchafalaya. With this age-old baffle suddenly removed, the river flowed much better. In fact, it flowed too well. For the Mississippi, which had for millennia accepted its own sluggish, winding path to the Gulf, was suddenly offered an enticingly shorter alternative into which it began sloughing off alarming quantities of water *(bottom left)*.

By the 20th Century, hydrologists realized that in time—and not too much time—the main trunk of the Mississippi would reroute itself into the Atchafalaya. New Orleans and Baton Rouge would find themselves on a swampy backwater. And the billions of dollars of freshwater-dependent industry in between them would be doomed.

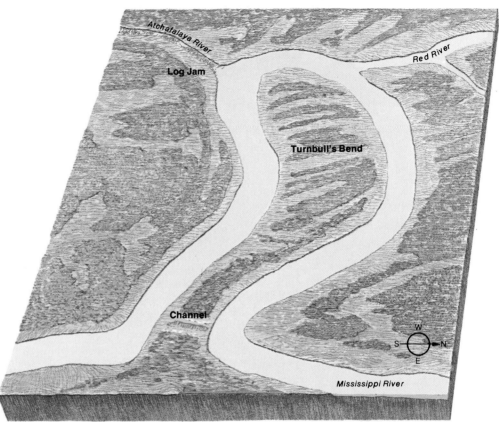

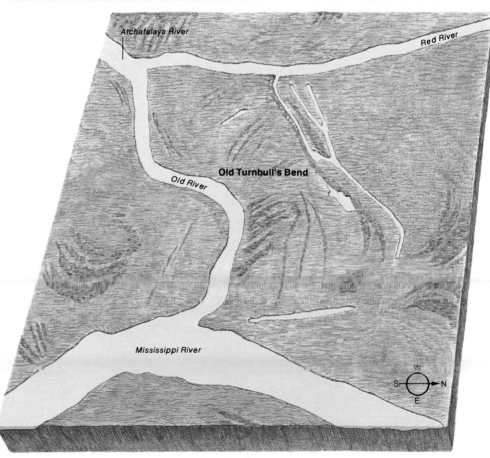

Red River

OUTFLOW
CHANNEL

Overbank
Structure

Low Sill Structure

Gantry Crane

By 1954, the possibility of losing the lower Mississippi became so alarming that Congress empowered the Army Corps of Engineers to do whatever was necessary to keep the Mississippi in its channel. The Corps's proposal—known as the Old River Control Project *(left)*—included an earthen closure across the eastern end of the Old River and a lock and navigational channel to pass traffic between the river systems.

But this was only a first step. To prevent the Old River from simply skirting the dam, the Corps moved a few miles upstream and dug a new channel between the Mississippi and the Red and Atchafalaya Rivers.

Called the outflow channel, the new watercourse was essentially an artificial recreation of the Old River. But the man-made channel had one salient advantage: Control devices could be installed before water was allowed to enter the channel. Eleven huge steel gates were mounted in the face of a concrete closure that was in turn secured by pilings reaching 90 feet into the ground. A gantry crane atop the low sill structure, as it was called, slid back and forth allowing each gate to be set at whatever aperture was deemed right for the moment.

Flanking the low sill structure, on slightly higher ground to the north, was an overbank structure that consisted of a longer series of smaller gates. This was the crucial flood-control device, for should the low sill structure be endangered by a flood, the overbank gates could regulate the excess water. To complete the system, a 25-mile network of levees was strung between these two structures and the Old River closure dam.

Put into operation in 1963, the Control Project performed as expected for a decade, but then experienced severe trouble. The low sill structure was extensively damaged in the great flood of 1973, and though repairs were made, two more years of high water strained the control to its limit.

In 1980 the Corps began building an auxiliary control—another series of spillway gates on a new channel—just to the south of the overtaxed low sill structure. The Corps was confident that this final measure would curtail the Mississippi's wanderlust. But there were some critics who felt that the Mississippi would inevitably follow the Old River and the Atchafalaya to the sea.

"It's going to happen," said Raphael Kazmann, professor of civil engineering at Louisiana State University. "We can delay it, but ultimately the river will take over. In the long run, man cannot win."

Joining the Mississippi River (*foreground*) to Lake Pontchartrain 30 miles above New Orleans, the Bonnet Carré Floodway forms an angular channel through which excess river water can be diverted into the lake, and thence into the Gulf of Mexico. A spillway structure, consisting of a weir with 350 individually operated bays (*center foreground*), controls the amount of water tapped into the lake. Behind the control structure, three railroads and a highway cross the floodway on trestles.

construction of levees went forward until by 1981 more than 1,600 miles of earthworks enclosed the main stream of the Mississippi; in addition, strong dikes were built out into the river itself at certain key bends to help direct the flow and close secondary channels when necessary. And it is on the tributaries that perhaps the most remarkable changes have taken place.

Although the Tennessee Valley Authority, born in the early 1930s, is known primarily as a power-producing enterprise, it also incorporates a major flood-control operation, affecting not only the Tennessee River but the lower Ohio and, consequently, the Mississippi. Eight reservoirs on the Tennessee and 10 on its tributaries can withhold some 12 million acre-feet of water. In February 1957, the Tennessee at Chattanooga would, by hydrologists' estimate, have reached a stage of 54 feet, the second highest level on record. Instead, thanks to the storage reservoirs, it peaked at a harmless 32.2 feet. Moreover, in May 1958, an estimated reduction of 3.1 feet in the stage of the Ohio-Mississippi at Cairo was attributed to the TVA control system.

Dwarfing all others in the sweep of its flood-control works is the mammoth project carried out since 1944 on the Missouri, where six huge dams are the keys to a 1,000-mile chain of 105 reservoirs capable of storing 75 million acre-feet of water, the largest water storage system in the United States. Within the basin, levees have been built to protect towns and farms. The dams themselves generate enough energy to meet the annual needs of the state of Nebraska.

The results are dramatically visible. For example, in 1943, the year before the plan was authorized, a fierce flood left Omaha's airport under seven feet of water; since then, although water in greater volume and with even more potential for damage has drained into the Missouri on at least four occasions, the airport has remained dry.

In the Ohio's basin, by 1979 more than $2.3 billion had been spent on flood control—but engineers reckoned that about $6.6 billion in flood damages had been saved, mostly by the 74 dam-formed lakes that impound the Ohio's tributary waters.

Among the most fascinating and important control systems is the one that operates on an odd little stream that joins the Mississippi about 80 miles above

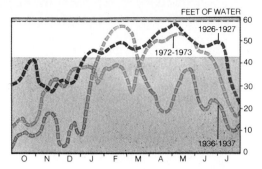

FEET OF WATER

1926-1927

1972-1973

1936-1937

O N D J F M A M J J

A hydrograph, the indispensable tool of hydrology, documents the monthly changes in water levels at Vicksburg, Mississippi, for the three worst flood periods of the century. While the 1927 and 1973 floods both have roughly the same profile, cresting in the month of May, the great inundation of 1937 makes its dramatic rise in January and February.

Louisiana's capital at Baton Rouge. The Old River is scarcely seven miles long, and connects the great river with the junction of the Red and Atchafalaya Rivers to the west. Historically, the Mississippi has struggled to adopt a new route to the sea along the Old River and the Atchafalaya. To prevent this dire eventuality, which would leave Baton Rouge and New Orleans stranded in a stagnant backwater, the Corps of Engineers has erected a massive series of spillways, floodways and levees in the area *(pages 83-85)*. The system is working, but it is a highly controversial project that some engineers expect to fail completely by early in the coming century.

For more than 200 years after men first started keeping records of the Mississippi's rise and fall, the river had averaged one flood every seven years. From 1950 to 1973, however, natural events and man-made controls combined to produce an eerie lull. That 23-year period of relative tranquillity—mistaken by some people as evidence that the river had at last been brought to leash—was shattered in 1973.

During the flood of 1973, water in incredible volume—more than 14 million gallons passing a given point at a given time—moved down the Mississippi. Nevertheless, at Cairo the river crested at only 55.7 feet, .7 foot lower than in 1927 and 3.8 feet lower than in the 1937 flood. At Vicksburg the crest was 53.1 feet, compared with 59.9 feet in 1927 and 57 feet in 1937. About 16.5 million acres in seven states were flooded and property losses were put at a staggering one billion dollars. Yet for all the destruction spread by the 1973 flood, it might have been much worse: Engineers estimated that flood-control works had prevented another 14.5 million acres from being inundated and had reduced damages from a possible $15 billion. As for the casualty figures, timely warnings and effective evacuation and rescue efforts resulted in only 23 dead—though 69,000 were rendered homeless in testimony to the Mississippi's still-untamed power. Ω

Although in principle a flood is a relatively straightforward phenomenon, to scientists it is infinitely and exasperatingly complex. Many important flood-control problems are literally insoluble by theoretical engineering, because mind-boggling equations dealing with dams, levees, revetments, soil characteristics and rainfall overwhelm even the most sophisticated computers. As a result, hydrologists and engineers throughout the world spend much of their time assembling a veritable Lilliput of working models—a watery world where they can actually observe hundreds of hypothetical floods.

Such experiments are particularly important in Japan, a country notoriously vulnerable to severe floods. Precipitation from the Pacific Ocean—winter snows, summer typhoons and frontal storms—washes the country with 70 inches of water per year, more than twice the U.S. average. And the rocky slopes of a 10,000-foot mountain range down the center of the long and narrow island chain supply short, steep rivers, which flood quickly and easily, bringing calamity to the country's densely populated low-lying urban areas.

As an aid in planning their flood defense, the Japanese rely on a sophisticated array of finely crafted models: rivers, dikes, dams, spillways and reservoirs. At Tsukuba Science City, northeast of Tokyo, various watershed models are flooded to identify the weakest points in the flood-control systems and to test complex spillway release schedules and other emergency tactics. In addition, watershed experiments help hydrologists predict the height of an actual flood crest from early rainfall reports, allowing timely evacuation of threatened areas.

Individual models are used for general design research into problems that plague engineers everywhere: minimizing reservoir sedimentation, reducing turbulence in the basin below a dam, controlling riverbed scour and erosion, or designing cheap but strong riprap, for example. These models also are used to address a less vital but equally difficult problem: how to adjust water temperature and oxygen content above and below dams to preserve the habitat for fish—and fishermen.

To chart river currents, two Japanese researchers pour brilliant streams of white and green dye into a working model of Tokyo's flood-prone Araka River. The 1,400-foot-long scale model allows engineers to evaluate experimentally the overall impact of complex flood-control programs.

At left, testing a proposed method of controlling dike erosion, a researcher covers a simulated riverbank with vinyl plastic. Below, 500 gallons of water per second go sluicing down the embankment. At right, after the 60-second test, researchers gauge the damage to the embankment by measuring down from horizontal strings. The plastic was washed away, along with much of the embankment, confirming that vinyl is an entirely inadequate riverbank reinforcement.

Below the spillway of a model dam, researchers use an electronic probe and a digital recorder to measure erosive turbulence in the outflow, an important consideration in dam design. The numbered lines on the spillway wall mark elevation; the ropes hanging in the background indicate the force and direction of downstream currents.

Above a miniature spillway a technician adjusts a dangling electronic probe that records the level achieved by different water-release rates. Such experiments allow engineers to tailor spillways to the water-flow characteristics of individual dams.

Researchers measure water conditions electronically at various locations along a zigzag-shaped river channel designed to damp the velocity and turbulence of water surging from a spillway. Without the baffled stilling basin, the spillway's cascade would quickly erode the downstream riverbed and might even double back to undermine the dam itself.

Inside a cavernous 250-foot-long "rain room,"
a researcher checks soil conditions in a simulated
downpour while the gauge at left monitors the
rainfall. The rainmaker, located 52 feet above the
floor, can mimic any type of rainstorm: Raindrop size
can be varied between $^1/_{10}$ and $^1/_{100}$ inch; rainfall
can range from $^1/_2$ inch to eight inches per hour.

In the control cab of the rain room, a computerized
strip recorder charts the amount of water that
percolates through the soil to a central drain—
data that hydrologists and meteorologists use
to forecast floods caused by saturated soil.

Chapter 4

FLOODS THAT COME IN A FLASH

It rains! Rapidly little rills are formed, and these soon grow into brooks, and the brooks grow into creeks and tumble over the canyon walls in innumerable cascades. The waters that fall during the rain, on those steep rocks, are gathered at once into the river; they could scarcely be poured in more suddenly if some vast spout ran from the clouds."

Exploring the canyon country of Colorado in 1869, Major John Wesley Powell had just witnessed one of those violent spasms of nature known today as flash floods. Swiftly expending its convulsive fury, Powell's flood subsided within minutes and the wasteland once more stood serene. Because the episode occurred in a place far removed from man's habitation, no damage was done to human life or property.

Flash floods, of course, remain unchanged in their elemental ferocity. But the chances that they will cause harm have been vastly increased by the spread of urban complexes and by the reach of civilization into areas previously remote. The United States alone experiences hundreds of flash floods annually, and the average number of people killed has risen to nearly 200—triple the average yearly toll of the 1940s. Indeed, says George P. Cressman, former director of the U.S. National Weather Service, "in this country, the flash flood has become the most dangerous weather phenomenon of them all."

There are no statistics on the number of flash floods worldwide each year, or on the enormity of the damage they cause. Their relative impact on life and livelihood can vary widely depending on climate and geography. Losses of life and property are especially high in Southeast Asia, where flash floods kill hundreds of people and destroy about 10 million acres of crops annually. A problem in many countries is population expansion into flood-prone areas. Many thousands of people have been killed in the floods that occur on an almost routine basis in the hills surrounding the Brazilian metropolis of Rio de Janeiro. One particularly bad flood took place in January 1967, when slides of mud and rock poured down hillsides and into the city itself, killing 864 people. A month later floods in the same area killed another 300.

Few regions on earth are entirely free from the peril. Only the most desiccated of deserts, where it rains scarcely at all—China's Gobi, the central Sahara, the Atacama Desert in northern Chile—are more or less immune to flash floods. Elsewhere, even in arid lands, when it rains it sometimes pours—and when it pours, there are flash floods, sudden and devastating.

North-central Iran receives on the average only eight inches of rain annually. Most of it falls in the winter and spring, and there can be some briefly fierce downpours. The effect on an unsuspecting—or unheeding—people can be

A mother and child perch precariously on the roof of their submerged automobile as the waters from a flash flood swirl around them near Yuba City, California, in December 1955. Trapped atop the car for seven hours, they were rescued by a helicopter soon after this photograph was snapped.

frightful. In the early hours of August 17, 1954, a savage thunderstorm hammered the town of Farahzad, located in the hills 30 miles northwest of Teheran. Normally dry creeks and ravines filled and swelled and joined in a great wall of water roaring down on the Muslim shrine of Imamzadeh Davoud. At the shrine were 3,000 pilgrims, who either did not hear or ignored the cry of a mullah to "run up the hillsides, for your lives." Instead, they remained at the shrine, where they prayed by candlelight. As a survivor recalled, a wall of water 90 feet high "smashed through the gates, tore off the roof, put out the candles, and swept through the area, carrying with it hundreds of stunned, mutilated, and drowning people." Rescue workers, who eventually reached the scene by donkey caravan, found more than 1,000 dead.

In underdeveloped nations, such as Iran, such disasters are viewed as inescapable, to be suffered as the immutable will of God. But in some nations with sophisticated weather monitoring and forecasting services—notably Japan,

The T. W. Ayers family of Heppner, Oregon, are seen in front of their home, decorated for a firemen's convention in May 1903. A few weeks later a flash flood on nearby Willow Creek destroyed the house (*right*) and drowned nine members of the family.

Canada and Britain—a powerful effort is under way to pinpoint the weather systems leading to flash floods and to warn endangered areas of their advance.

Nowhere is the campaign being waged with greater intensity than in the United States. Against the dire and rising threat of flash floods, the National Weather Service since 1970 has tried to achieve what had long been considered impossible. "The idea that we might be able to spot impending flash floods and give adequate warning was simply beyond imagining," recalls Charles Smith, hydrologist in charge at the Weather Service's Northeast River Forecasting Center at Bloomfield, Connecticut. "Then we began to realize that our improved technology might make it worth a try and that we could perhaps save lives. We've had some success, but we still have an awfully long way to go."

By their very nature, flash floods all too frequently defy the most sensitive arrays of equipment and the best predictive capabilities of man's mind. The National Weather Service definition of a flash flood is one that occurs within a few hours after the storm that spawns it. But the fact is that flash floods often build up much more rapidly—as witness the fate that befell Heppner, Oregon, on June 14, 1903. Between 4 and 5 p.m., a wild thunderstorm drenched the basin of little Willow Creek in the foothills of the Blue Mountains. Within half an hour the creek was out of its banks and roaring toward Heppner, which lay squarely in its path. Scarcely 60 minutes after the first raindrops fell, the storm, and the flood, were all over. Yet in that speck of time, 247 of Heppner's 1,400 people had died.

Aside from the bewildering speed with which they strike, flash floods can confound forecasters because the weather systems that create them are typically of small rather than large magnitude. Most often, the danger arises when stationary or very slow-moving thunderclouds unload huge amounts of water onto the areas over which they happen to be hanging.

The phenomenon, popularly known as a cloudburst, is generally triggered by changes—which can be minute and virtually undetectable—in upward air currents. The consistency of water is such that the maximum speed of a falling raindrop in still air is about 17 miles per hour; if it goes any faster it breaks up into mist. By the same token, if air currents are rising at more than 17 miles an

The second story and cupola are all that remain of the Ayers' home after the flood, which carried the building six blocks from its original location. The deadly waters swept away one third of Heppner's buildings and killed 247 out of a population of 1,400.

hour they inhibit rain from falling, and clouds become airborne reservoirs for enormous accumulations of moisture. Then, if the updrafts suddenly diminish, the overburdened clouds burst open, dumping their entire contents in one great gush over a relatively small area, often less than 20 square miles.

The prodigious problem for the forecasters is to identify which clouds among an oncoming rank of thunderstorms have cloudburst potential. The forecasters then have to predict if and when the cloudburst will take place—and translate the whole into an appraisal of danger that takes into consideration the topography and population density below. A possible cloudburst over a section of flat, sparsely populated plain is obviously less alarming than one over hilly country with towns and cities nestled in river valleys.

Confronted by a phenomenon of bewildering complexity, the Weather Service has responded with an intricate, interlaced system for collecting, analyzing and disseminating the weather information that goes into flash-flood forecasts. The National Meteorological Center at Camp Springs, Maryland, is responsible for tracking and interpreting worldwide weather developments and for feeding its findings to the 13 river forecasting centers that are the heart of the network. Each river forecasting center covers a vast tract of the United States; the Bloomfield, Connecticut, installation, for example, encompasses 100,000 square miles, including the six New England states and most of New York.

Unlike the Camp Springs facility, which is staffed by meteorologists concerned with atmospheric conditions that may (or may not) result in precipitation, the river centers employ hydrologists who are mainly concerned with what the water might do after it hits the ground. These experts have primary jurisdiction over flood forecasts and warnings issued for the streams and watersheds within their domain.

To carry out that assignment the river forecasting centers receive not only the qualitative data provided by the National Meteorological Center but quantitative information—the actual amounts of precipitation either expected or already falling—from 52 Weather Service forecast offices and 250 Weather Service offices. The Weather Service forecast offices generally have state-wide responsibilities while the Weather Service offices are more local in focus. Besides reporting to the river forecasting centers, the Weather Service forecast offices and the Weather Service offices disseminate to affected communities the forecasts and warnings prepared by the river center hydrologists.

To assist them in their awesome task, the forecasters are armed with a dazzling array of ultramodern technological tools. Yet such are the vagaries and the variables of flash-flood prediction that even the most sophisticated equipment is often inadequate—and the lines of organizational responsibility, which appear so tidy on paper, frequently blur. In such cases, the last line of defense is human instinct and individual judgment—and both are admittedly fallible.

One measure of the discouragements can be found in the fact that the calamity that helped inspire the Weather Service to its flash-flood warning efforts might be as unpredictable today as it was on the tragic night it occurred.

"The devil himself couldn't have produced a more unlikely series of freakish events with more perfect timing to cause such a concentrated torrential rainfall," said a National Weather Service official in the aftermath of the terrible storm. It happened on the night of August 19, 1969, in the Blue Ridge Mountain country southwest of Charlottesville, Virginia—and resulted in the worst natural disaster in the annals of the state.

Tuesday, August 19, was a sullen, sultry day; a warm, moist mass of air from the Atlantic hung low and almost motionless over the hills and hollows of Nelson County. That afternoon the remnants of Hurricane Camille moved over Kentucky and West Virginia, depositing a relatively meager two to four inches of rain as it went. One of history's great tempests, Camille had savaged the coast along the Gulf of Mexico, then slashed northward, leaving behind it a broad swath of destruction. Now, veering east toward Virginia and the Atlantic, the storm was dying.

At about the same time, the National Weather Service warned the Washington, D.C., area of the approach of a cold front preceded by a line of thunderstorms. As it happened, the system skirted Washington and headed south—toward a fateful collision with the stagnant mass of maritime air and the decaying remains of Camille. As darkness fell, a 52-year-old Nelson County resident, Ivanhoe Stevens, uneasily watched the gathering of the elements: "From every angle that you looked, these clouds were rolling, just in a roll, and they were coming to a peak right in the top of the sky, just like a hornet's nest. I'd never seen clouds roll together like that."

Pouring eastward over the Blue Ridge barrier, Camille's center actually passed north of Nelson County, but the hurricane's counterclockwise winds picked up wet air from the Atlantic and from the clouds already hovering overhead. The winds pushed the combined air masses through the steeply constricted valleys of the Rockfish and the Tye Rivers, compressing the moisture. The arrival of the cold air from the north was a catalyst for cloudburst.

The rain began about 9:30 p.m. and it came in a volume meteorologists later

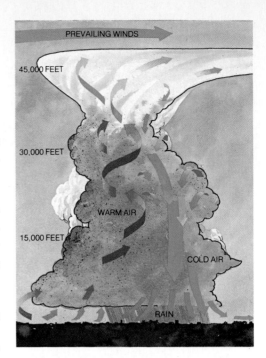

As a severe thunderstorm starts to develop, masses of low-lying, warm, humid air are sent swirling upward by an atmospheric disturbance and condense into a billowing cloud. When the cloud rises to around 50,000 feet its ascent is checked and a white, anvil-shaped cap appears, blown horizontally by prevailing winds; rain begins to fall, producing downdrafts that will eventually dissipate the cloud.

The U.S. flash-flood warning system is depicted in this chart. Atmospheric data are fed from radar, satellite, and surface and upper air observation devices to the National Meteorological Center near Washington, D.C., to regional river forecasting centers, and to state and local weather-forecast offices. The national and regional agencies give precipitation and runoff guidance to the state and local forecasters, who issue flash-flood watches and warnings to various action groups for dissemination to the public.

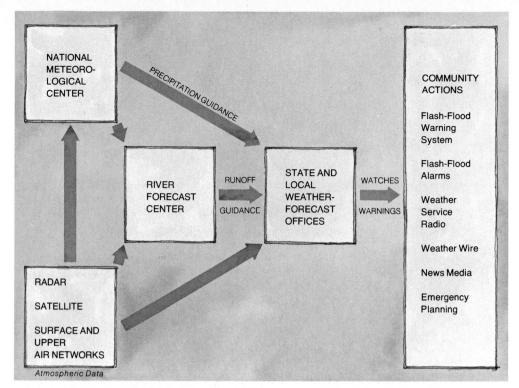

calculated as likely to occur in that area once in 1,000 years. "Rain wasn't falling in no drops," recalled Stevens. "It was just a solid sheet of water."

The 471 square miles of Nelson County were swamped. At one measuring station a fantastic 31.5 inches of rain was reported during a six-hour period; the county as a whole averaged 18 inches. In all, an estimated 1.2 trillion gallons of water crashed down upon the luckless county, bloating the Rockfish River, which rose by 27 feet, and forcing such small mountain streams as Muddy Creek, Davis Creek and Hat Creek to burst from their banks and rage in scores of flash floods throughout the afflicted countryside.

Nelson County was peculiarly vulnerable to the onslaught. Although a place of surpassing beauty, it was scantily populated—the last census had numbered about 12,000 persons, mostly mountain farmers whose families had tended their small apple orchards and harvested their patches of hay in the area for as many as six generations. The living was hard—the county's median income was only $3,088—and communications between the isolated farmsteads were poor. The flash floods, coming as they did in the night and early morning—roughly between 9:30 p.m. and 3:30 a.m.—struck victims who were entirely unaware of their imminent doom. "Even if we had some warning," a Nelson County official said later, "there was no way we could have gotten word to our people. Everybody was in bed with radios and televisions turned off, and the mud and water came too fast for neighbors to warn one another."

The peril was compounded by the geology of the region. A team from the U.S. Geological Survey later reported: "On the eastern slopes of the Blue Ridge, the soil is underlain directly by rather impervious igneous and metamorphic rocks." The rain and the floods that surged across the surface "quickly saturated the soil, increasing the weight of the soil layer, decreasing the cohesive shear strength of the soil, and lubricating the layer." In an area that bordered the main north-south highway through the county, continued the report, "a whole section of the mountainside suddenly gave way and slid down, aided by the steep slope angle. All the vegetation, including large trees, and much of the soil was stripped away in scars that in many places exposed bedrock."

Ripped up by their roots, scraped naked of their bark by the grinding action of water and rock, their branches torn and trunks splintered, thousands of trees were carried along by the avalanches of water and mud. On a night illuminated

The Mouse That Marred Operation Foresight

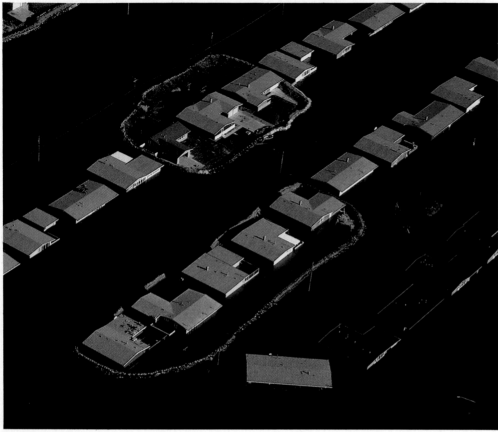

Two islands of homes in Minot, North Dakota, bear testimony to the frantic efforts of householders to protect their property from the floodwaters of the Mouse River in April 1969. When last-minute word reached Minot that the Mouse was rising, these homeowners hastily pooled their resources and hired a bulldozer to throw up earth dikes around their houses. The dike at top held; the one below did not.

In January 1969 the National Weather Service's river forecasting center in Kansas City, Missouri, began issuing long-range advisory notices that boded ill for riverside towns in Minnesota and in the Dakotas.

Satellite pictures, backed up by wide-ranging ground patrols, had revealed an ominous flood hazard. Across thousands of square miles of frozen prairie lay a blanket of snow four feet thick—three times the normal seasonal amount. By February the snow's moisture content was extremely high—equal to six to 10 inches of water. If there was an early spring and a sudden thaw, the entire region could be inundated.

To combat the threat, the U.S. Office of Emergency Preparedness initiated a massive campaign, called Operation Foresight, at federal, state and local government levels. Flood-fighting experts were sent into the region to help authorities build emergency levees along critical streams. The U.S. Army Corps of Engineers blasted apart ice jams in the rivers to drain off as much water as possible prior to the spring melt. Pumps were provided for such vital facilities as hospitals and police stations. Provi-

sions were stockpiled at critical locations.

In early April, just as the river forecasting center had feared, the Red River, the Big Sioux, the Minnesota, the Blue Earth and others—3,700 miles of rivers in all—came into spate and sent a total volume of water racing downstream that doubled the previous flood record.

But thanks to Operation Foresight, damage was moderate—everywhere except in Minot, North Dakota, a town with a population of 33,000 on the banks of the narrow, 435-mile-long Mouse River, which looped south from Saskatchewan, Canada. There had been no serious flooding on the Mouse or on any of its tributaries for more than 40 years. Consequently—and as things turned out, tragically—Minot had been excluded from the flood alert and from Operation Foresight.

On Easter, April 6, the citizens of Minot had only a few hours' notice before the Mouse overflowed its banks and came rushing into town. Mercifully no one was killed, but the floodwaters wiped out one third of all the homes, 212 stores and offices, 15 churches and two schools.

only by lightning, Curtis Matthews of Wood's Mill recognized the odor of raw green wood: "I'm in the logging business and know that smell, but I had never in my life smelled it so heavy, even in a sawmill. The air was thick with it every breath you took. It was like sticking your head in a sack of bark." Matthews roused the family; they fled before the oncoming wall of water and timber and had just made it to safety when the flood roared over their homestead.

A gray and dismal dawn disclosed a scene of desolation through the area. Of the 465 miles of roadway in Nelson County, 135 were completely destroyed and 50 were damaged. Homes, farms and village streets lay buried under as much as 30 feet of mud and debris. Along a 200-foot stretch of road near Roseland, a flash flood had piled boulders up to 10 feet in diameter; in some areas, rescue operations could be carried out only by helicopter.

Nelson County lost 125 people during the night. Many drowned, but others were crushed by boulders, mutilated by flood-tossed trees or engulfed by mud. One man and his wife were found trapped in mud up to their necks. The woman was already dead, and her husband died before rescue workers could dig down to his knees. Along Davis Creek, normally no more than a few inches deep, the bodies of 14 members of the Huffman family were identified; five other Huffmans were never found. And 80 days after the floods had subsided, the corpse of a man was excavated from beneath 12 feet of sand, in which it had been perfectly preserved.

In the inquiries that followed the floods, it was agreed that the National Weather Service was unprepared to foresee the fantastic rainfall that led to Nelson County's ordeal. And because the Weather Service was determined not to suffer another such embarrassment, the tragedy of Nelson County became a turning point for attempts to forecast sudden floods.

In late 1969, soon after the Nelson County catastrophe, the Weather Service began issuing watch and warning bulletins for flash floods, just as it had long done for tornadoes. The early efforts were exasperating. High hopes were held for the Geostationary Operational Environmental Satellites, operated by the National Oceanic and Atmospheric Administration at a fixed position 22,300 miles above the Equator; the satellites became operational in 1975 and proved effective at tracking major weather systems. Moreover, promising experiments were under way using satellite sensors to measure cloudtop temperature to aid quantitative as well as qualitative forecasting: The colder its top the more likely a cloud is to produce rain in amounts that might cause flash flooding.

But the satellites left much to be desired in their ability to detect the relative pinpoints that characterize medium-sized storms. And, considering the speed with which such storms can form and strike, too much time was lost analyzing and interpreting satellite findings.

Similarly, the radar with which various Weather Service stations were equipped proved of limited value. Radar estimates of rainfall rates are based on the intensity of the echo received by the station from the affected area. Given ideal conditions, forecasters could scan their radarscopes and tell, with considerable confidence, just how much rain was descending upon a specific area. But radar's accuracy decreases with distance, and the outside range of the weather radar then in existence was about 125 miles. In addition, the radar was subject to distortion by, among other things, the interference of the rain itself if it happened to be pelting down on the radar station and its antenna.

Even when satellites and radar lived up to the Weather Service's fondest hopes, the information they provided had to be given specific application. To the flash-flood hydrologists in the river forecasting centers, the problem boiled down to a single, crucial question: How much rain would it take to cause flooding at a certain place at a particular time under a given set of conditions? By 1970, the answers existed for many critical areas, stored in the memory banks of computers. Scores of factors were involved, including the past behavior patterns of specific streams, the slopes of their channels and valleys, the permeability of the ground in their watersheds, the extent to which the soil might recently have been soaked and the density of vegetation in their drainage basins.

Given such variables, the hydrologists, simply by punching a few computer keys, could find out what would probably happen if, say, the drainage area of a specific stream received four inches of rain in two hours. The chief difficulty, of course, lay in supplying the computers with sufficient information on a nation-wide scale. Almost any stream will rise swiftly, given enough rain in a short enough period. And tens of thousands of streams around the United States carried a potential for trouble. Millions of factual bits and pieces were involved, and the task of collecting them was almost endless.

Thus, throughout the 1970s and into the 1980s, the state of the infant science of flash-flood forecasting was such that it depended heavily on a picket line of individual sentinels—both human and mechanical. For the on-the-scene reports vital to forecasters, the Weather Service employed a small army of 12,000 observers, some of them paid nominal amounts for their service but most of them volunteers. In wilderness watersheds, on creeks meandering through rural countryside or flowing through the concrete jungles of great American cities, the observers checked precipitation and stream-stage gauges and reported their findings to Weather Service forecasters.

The system had obvious weaknesses. The observers performed their duties mostly during the day—but many of the convective storms that produce flash floods occurred at night. Being human, observers fell ill, took vacations, or simply tired of their jobs. Because of such difficulties, the Weather Service placed increasing emphasis on gauges requiring no human help (*opposite*).

Some gauges were linked to telephones that, when called by a forecaster, emitted signals that could be translated into precipitation or river-stage readings. Other gauges could, in effect, be phoned by computers that displayed the consequent readings on screens or print-outs. Still others sent their readings to one of the geostationary satellites at regular intervals or when rainfall or rivers reached dangerous levels. In particularly threatened areas of the United States, the Weather Service operated gauges that automatically sounded alarms in nearby communities whenever stream stages approached danger levels.

Yet the more sophisticated the gauge, the more vulnerable it was to technical failure: For example, the telephone lines that connected a gauge to a forecasting office could break during a severe storm. The most reliable gauge remained the simple, inexpensive type that consisted of little more than a container and a measuring stick and was checked by a human observer.

The Weather Service effort to develop a dependable flash-flood forecasting system was thus a long, frustrating process—a fact that was dismally demonstrated in 1976, seven years after the Nelson County tragedy and more than a century after Major John Wesley Powell explored the Colorado territory.

Colorado's Big Thompson River belies its name: It is in fact a tinkly little stream, rarely more than two feet deep, that tumbles down steep slopes from its Rocky Mountain headwaters toward its junction with the South Platte River, 78 miles to the east. During the first 21 miles of its course, the Big Thompson descends by about 5,000 feet before it reaches the town of Estes Park; two miles east of Estes Park the river sluices into the 25-mile-long gorge of Big Thompson Canyon, within whose narrow confines it falls another 2,500 feet before leveling off for its final 30-mile run to the South Platte.

Approximately 600 persons live year-round in the wilderness area of Big Thompson Canyon. However, Saturday, July 31, 1976, marked the beginning of a three-day weekend celebrating the 100th anniversary of Colorado's admittance to the Union. Motels and campgrounds were crammed to capac-

Measuring water, whether it is falling from the sky or coursing down a boulder-strewn ravine, is a complex process. Yet for meteorologists as much as for any scientist, precise measurement is the indispensable first step toward understanding the ways of nature.

The billions of gallons of water that rain to earth have traditionally been measured in terms of height. A pan set outside during a midsummer's downpour might collect half an inch of water in an afternoon, but to obtain a finer degree of measurement—the hydrologist's unit of measure in the United States is a hundredth of an inch—a more sophisticated device is needed.

The simplest scientific rain gauge, used around the world by weather services, is a pan-funnel-cylinder device *(below, left)* that allows the observer to make his measurement by means of a calibrated dipstick. Although these simple gauges are extremely accurate, they cannot be hooked up to automatic recording devices that would permit meteorologists to monitor rainfall simultaneously over a broad area. To accomplish this, weathermen depend on more complicated devices.

The two most common are the weighing-type gauge *(below, right)* and the tipping-bucket gauge *(below, center)*. Both types are wired into telephone lines so that weathermen can record rainfall in remote areas simply by dialing the gauge's number and listening to a coded signal. These gauges can also be programed to initiate a call to the weather bureau should flood conditions suddenly arise.

Recently, in the United States, many gauges have been equipped with radio transmitters that bounce rainfall data off satellites so that hour by hour changes in precipitation—and potential flash-flood situations—all over the country can be watched from one central location.

Once the rain has fallen, however, a new problem arises: measuring the water that collects in streams and rivers. For this, scientists turn to an old and trusted measuring device, illustrated on the following pages, called the stilling well.

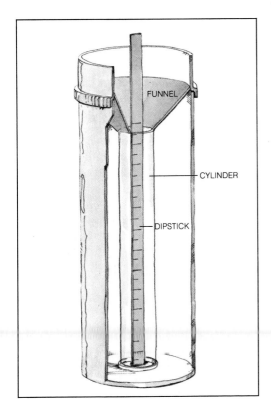

The mouth of the central cylinder of the simple pan-funnel-cylinder rain gauge is exactly ¹/₁₀ the area of the mouth of the collecting pan above it. Thus it exaggerates the vertical dimension of the water that is collected by exactly 10 times, allowing a precise measurement in hundredths of an inch to be read from a specially calibrated dipstick.

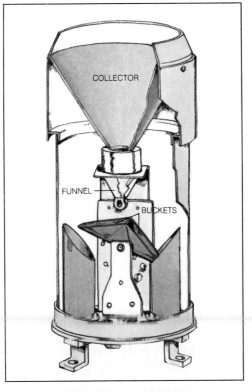

Two tiny triangular buckets, each able to hold exactly ¹/₁₀₀ inch of water, pivot on a seesaw underneath a collecting pan drained through a small funnel. One bucket fills with water until it tips, spilling its load and bringing the other bucket into position under the funnel. Each tip triggers an electromagnetic pulse that can be recorded on a monitoring device.

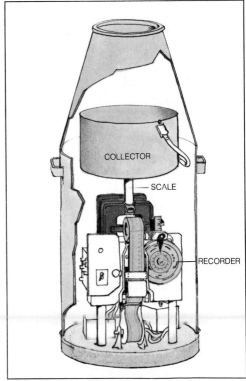

A collecting bucket is mounted on a delicate spring scale that is used to weigh the water that accumulates through the opening in the cover of the rain gauge. The scale is calibrated to convert units of weight into hundredths of an inch, and a digital recorder that is attached to the right side of the scale keeps track of these readings.

A stilling well stands at a strategic spot along the Susquehanna River near Harrisburg, Pennsylvania. The well house of this river measuring device, connected to high ground by a bridge, holds the recording and communication systems *(bottom);* an observer can be stationed in the house, or the recording devices can be operated automatically.

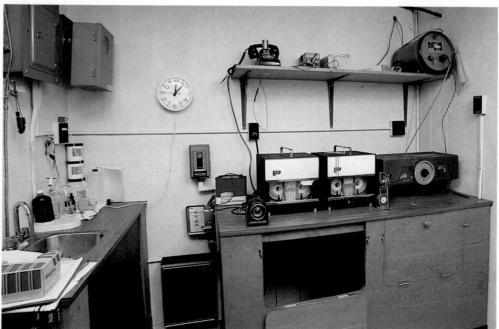

A change of a quarter of an inch in stage—the height of water in a stream at a given point—can be a critical factor in predicting the likelihood of a disastrous flood. However, to make a measurement this fine on the ordinarily turbulent surface of a river is virtually impossible without the help of a device known as a stilling well, shown in cross section above.

Essentially a sealed hole dug adjacent to the river and connected to it by underground pipes, the stilling well will fill to exactly the same height as the river. But the water, protected from wind and currents, will be smooth, still and easy to measure. This measurement is usually made in the instrument house above the well by means of a float suspended from an automatic recording device, which tracks the most minute changes in water level 24 hours a day. In winter the well house is heated to prevent the water from freezing and thus causing an exaggerated measurement.

ity, bringing the total number of people in the canyon's vicinity to 3,500.

The daily forecast, as issued by the Weather Service forecast office in Denver, about 50 miles south of Big Thompson Canyon, called for widely scattered showers. Among the tools at the disposal of the Denver forecaster were satellite reports relayed by the Satellite Field Service Station in Kansas City, Missouri, facsimiles of readings from a weather radar station at Limon, Colorado, and precipitation information from law enforcement agencies, volunteer and paid observers, and automated gauges in the field.

Late that afternoon a line of thunderstorms formed from central Kansas to eastern Colorado—setting in motion a series of human and technological failures with terrible consequences. Hardly had the storms developed when they stalled, thunderheads hanging almost motionless from their anvil-shaped tops at 60,000 feet. Then the line of thunderheads began to deteriorate at both ends, growing weaker and weaker until only a 12-mile-wide band of intense activity remained—spread from Estes Park to the town of Drake. Between 5:30 and 6 p.m. a soft sprinkle began to fall on Estes Park. It was the harbinger of an intense rainstorm that began at about 6:30 and within the next four and a half hours loosed more than 12 inches of water, nearly all of it on the western, or upper, one third of Big Thompson Canyon.

In Denver the lead forecaster was already being deprived, one by one, of his predictive resources. The Satellite Field Service Station in Kansas City was of no help whatever. The two satellite specialists on duty were entirely preoccupied with watching large, menacing storm systems develop in the southern Mississippi River basin and over Missouri and Arkansas. They paid scant attention to the smaller, seemingly less dangerous thunderstorm activity that had appeared within Denver's region.

Similarly, the radar information received from the Limon installation was of meager assistance. Since Limon and Big Thompson Canyon were separated by about 115 miles, near the outer edge of radar's effectiveness, the readings received by Limon were somewhat suspect.

In any event, the video transmitting equipment that might have provided Denver with facsimiles of Limon's radar findings was shut down for repairs. Although the operator at Limon tried to describe his readings by telephone, the Denver forecaster was, in the words of a subsequent disaster report, "unable to fully grasp the situation as the radar was viewing it."

At 7:35 p.m., the Denver forecaster issued a severe thunderstorm warning, and added at the end of the bulletin the possibility that "there could be some flooding of low areas." To spread word of such bulletins, the Weather Service relies heavily on news media. But in this case the Associated Press, for reasons that remain unexplained, did not put the limited warning on its wires until 9:07 p.m.; at least one radio station continued in its play-by-play account of a football game without interrupting for the weather bulletin, and a television station failed to show so much as a weather "crawler" across the bottom of its screen during the showing of a movie.

After issuing his 7:35 report, the Denver forecaster was uneasy about the scantiness of the information he had been able to collect. For first-hand data he looked to a roster of observers enlisted by the Weather Service. Unhappily, during the previous two years the Weather Service had been severely hampered by budget restrictions placed on the travel expenses required to recruit and train such observers. The local reporting system had fallen into sad disarray and no observers reported from the threatened area.

Moreover, as it was later learned, the only automated rain gauge in Big Thompson Canyon was evidently malfunctioning—it sent erroneous radio signals and was, in the event, washed away by the flood. An hour passed, and the Denver forecaster's malaise continued to grow, though he received no new information. At 9 p.m., acting largely on intuition, he sent out another no-

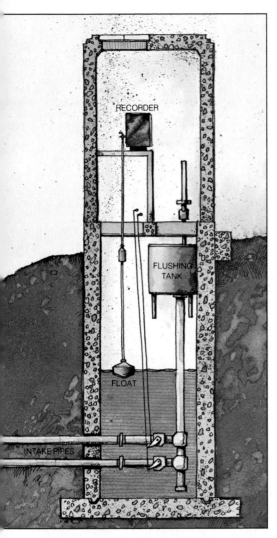

Digital recorders, like the one above and the two on the counter in the well house at left, trace changes in water level at 15-minute intervals by punching holes in a paper tape. This data can then be relayed via telephone or radio to a flood forecast center.

tice: THUNDERSTORMS ARE MOVING SLOWLY WHICH COULD RESULT IN SOME LOCAL FLOODING.

It was already too late.

The downpour in the neighborhood of the Big Thompson Canyon increased until, as a Colorado state trooper later recalled, "raindrops a half-inch in diameter were coming straight down. My slicker pockets filled with water almost instantly." Shortly after 8 o'clock the Colorado Highway Patrol office at Greeley, 43 miles east of Estes Park, received a telephone report of a washout on U.S. Highway 34, a scenic route that passes through Big Thompson Canyon alongside the river. The Greeley dispatcher sent trooper William Miller, who had been on duty near Estes Park, into the canyon to investigate. From then on, events happened too fast for the highway patrol even to think of notifying the Weather Service of the calamity in the making.

At 8:35 Miller reported from a position seven and a half miles within the canyon: "We've got to start taking people out. My car's gonna be washed away. I've got a real emergency down here." He did indeed, and seconds later his voice rose to a shout: "The whole mountainside is gone. There is no way. I'm trying to get out of here before I drown."

Miller swam to high ground—but another trooper, Sergeant Hugh Purdy, was less fortunate. At about 9:15 Purdy radioed: "I'm stuck. I'm right in the middle of it. I can't get out." His battered body was later found eight miles downstream from the spot where he had made his final call.

Engorged by the rainstorm, the Big Thompson River had risen by 20 feet in some places, and it raced through the canyon at a velocity estimated at more than 20 feet per second. One survivor recalled: "Campers were being washed away and big propane tanks were coming downstream, spinning like crazy, starting to explode." Another survivor saw Highway 34 ripping apart, "sending 10- or 12-foot chunks of asphalt high into the air."

Bursting from the canyon's mouth, the flood poured forth water in a volume that was later calculated at 233,000 gallons per second, smashing everything it encountered. Amid the debris found the following day was a motel register listing the names of 23 guests. None of them were found—and the motel itself was gone.

Not until shortly before 11 p.m. did the Denver forecaster finally receive word from the scene. Then and only then did he put out the warning that, had it been issued a few hours earlier, might have saved some lives: A FLASH FLOOD WARNING IS IN EFFECT UNTIL 4 AM MDT FOR PERSONS NEAR THE BIG THOMPSON RIVER. A FLASH FLOOD WARNING MEANS FLOODING IS IMMINENT.

These color-enhanced radar echoes from the Limon, Colorado, weather station show the progress of the cloudburst that triggered a deadly flash flood in Big Thompson Canyon on July 31, 1976. Operating at the limit of its 125-mile range, the radar accurately delineated the general area of rainfall *(green zone),* but underestimated the areas of heaviest downpour *(red zone).* Two to five inches fell per hour—about five times the predicted amount.

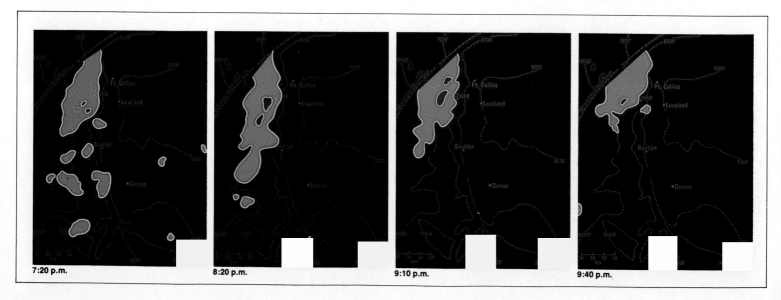

7:20 p.m.   8:20 p.m.   9:10 p.m.   9:40 p.m.

The Big Thompson disaster came about largely because of inadequacies and fateful breakdowns in the flash-flood forecasting system. The Denver forecaster might have salvaged something from the situation had he put out a stronger flood warning with the first severe-thunderstorm advisory at 7:35 p.m. He did not because he had no hard information to justify it—and because in those days, the Weather Service was extremely sensitive to the charge of issuing false alarms. "For a long while," recalls Charles Smith, a veteran Weather Service hydrologist, "we were so afraid of taking any chances that we issued flash-flood watch and warning bulletins when the situation really didn't warrant them. We cried 'wolf' so often that we lost credibility."

The dimensions of that loss of credibility were tragically illustrated in 1977 when, despite faultless forecasting, a Kansas City flash flood caused needless deaths because many citizens simply ignored the warnings.

Amid the phalanxes of computers and teleprinters and maps in their 17th-floor headquarters in Kansas City's downtown Federal Building, forecasters saw trouble coming as early as the morning of Sunday, September 11, 1977. Because a mass of warm, moist air from the south was moving toward a meeting with a cold mass from the west, the forecasters at 10:30 a.m. predicted a 70 per cent chance of thunderstorms for that night and the next day.

The storm hit shortly after midnight on September 12, and during the next six hours it soaked the area with about six inches of rain, causing some generally harmless flooding of small streams. More significantly, it saturated local drainage basins, decreasing their capacity to absorb more water and lowering the flash-flood index—the amount of rainfall in a three-hour period that, based on past records, is theoretically needed to produce minor floods in the area. Around Kansas City, the index dropped from four inches for September 11 to 1.6 for the next day. With this in mind, the Weather Service at 10:30 a.m. on Monday, September 12, issued a flash-flood watch for that afternoon and night.

Despite its critical importance, the difference between a flash-flood watch and a flash-flood warning is little understood by the public at which both are aimed. A watch means that weather conditions are developing that may lead to heavy rain and resulting floods. A warning means that flash floods are either imminent or have already begun; persons entering the area covered by a warning do so at their peril.

That afternoon a bright sun broke through overcast skies and the threat seemed over—to everyone but the forecasters, who already had satellite information indicating that another storm system was in the making.

The raw satellite information was received by Kansas City's Satellite Service Station at half-hour intervals from the Weather Service's Washington, D.C., headquarters. It came in the form of photographic images sent over telephone lines, photos that the Kansas City experts translated into moving-loop television pictures for a better sense of the storm's development.

The pictures, which the satellite-station analysts shared with the Kansas City forecasters, showed a thin line of cumulus clouds—a narrow band of energy that could set off explosive thunderstorm activity—advancing northward toward a junction near Topeka, Kansas, with a cold-air mass moving in from the west. At 1 p.m. a severe thunderstorm warning was issued for the Topeka area.

By late that afternoon, Kansas City radar was receiving precipitation echoes from a storm whose center was north of the metropolitan area. Only seven months before, the Weather Service had started using a scale of 1 to 6 by which to correlate the levels of intensity of radar echoes with actual amounts of rainfall. Radar Level 1 represented less than .2 inch of rain per hour; Level 2 represented .2 to 1.1 inches per hour, and so on until the bright echoes of Level 6 indicated torrential rain in amounts greater than 7.1 inches per hour.

By 5:30 p.m. several Level 5 echoes—4.5 to 7.1 inches per hour—had been

U.S. Highway 34 ends in a washout at the mouth of Colorado's Big Thompson Canyon after the 1976 flash flood. The flood also destroyed the supports of the Horsetooth Reservoir drain pipe, sending the 225,000-pound steel pipe 600 yards downstream, where it came to rest on the bank at upper left.

received from the area north and west of Kansas City. At 5:45 a flash-flood warning was issued for one county in Kansas and two in Missouri, all clustered northwest of Kansas City; at 6:45 the warning was extended to four Missouri counties just to the east of Kansas City. But at 7:30, satellite infrared images showed that the center of the storm had suddenly veered southward—toward Kansas City itself. Fifteen minutes later the Weather Service warned of flash floods in Jackson County, which includes much of the city.

In accordance with established procedure, the alarm was aired on the Weather Service's own VHF radio station and sent out by teleprinter to television and radio newsrooms; cooperating fully, all stations interrupted their regular programing to broadcast the bulletin.

Heavy rain began to fall on Kansas City at about 8 o'clock, almost immediately washing out a major league baseball game; several persons in the crowd would leave the stadium and drive to their deaths. By 8:06 reports were already being received of cars stalled in the streets. At 8:45 the Weather Service sent out a "Special Statement" of extraordinary urgency: THESE LATEST RAINS ARE PRODUCING A VERY DANGEROUS PROBLEM TO MOTORISTS AND PERSONS IN LOW LYING AREAS. DO NOT TAKE THIS SITUATION LIGHTLY AS IT IS POTENTIALLY VERY DANGEROUS TO LIFE AND PROPERTY.

Masked against the stench, a Colorado sheriff's deputy recovers the battered body of a baby from debris after the Big Thompson flood. The child drowned, along with her mother and grandmother, when the waters swept away their car. Because of pungent odors from dead animals, bloodhounds could not help search for victims; each pile of debris had to be picked apart individually.

During the next six hours another six to seven inches of rain would fall on Kansas City. Just like the storm that had afflicted the city earlier that day, the second downpour was a 100-year event—and for two such deluges to strike exactly the same area within 24 hours was a 1,000-year occurrence. Hardest hit was Brush Creek, a little stream scarcely worthy of the name.

Rising just across the state line in Kansas, Brush Creek drains a tiny area of 29.4 square miles and travels only 11 miles before entering the Big Blue River in Missouri. During its brief course it runs through Kansas City's Country Club Plaza, started in 1922 as the nation's first planned shopping center and now a complex of elegant boutiques, restaurants, hotels and apartment buildings.

Back in the 1930s a political boss, who happened to own a cement company, lined four miles of Brush Creek's bed with concrete while lining his own pockets with cash. Ever since, during the frequent periods when the stream runs dry, the paved bed has been used by bicyclists, by joggers and even for outdoor concerts; on the other hand, when water is in the creek the concrete makes an impermeable sluiceway. And local topography adds to the flood hazard. According to one hydrologist: "It's a flashy stream. It can be up and down in a matter of hours. Brush Creek slopes about 20 feet every mile. That's steep."

On that fatal night of September 12, Brush Creek rose by no less than 22 feet, bursting out of its bed, over its grassy banks and onto its flood plain—where lay the Country Club Plaza. In its greatest flow, the stream achieved an estimated 261,800 gallons per second—almost the same that its huge neighbor, the Missouri River, discharges during the navigational season. As at Big Thompson a year earlier, the creek's peak velocity was about 20 feet a second, seven times more than it takes to knock a person off his feet and more than enough to tumble a car.

By now, the forecasters in the Federal Building had accomplished all that they could reasonably be expected to do; they could only hope that the public would heed the warnings, which had been issued with time to spare and in terms of unmistakable urgency.

It was not to be. Despite the warnings, crowds in plaza restaurants and bars were normal for a Monday night. In one tippling place, customers looked out the windows, saw Brush Creek's surging waters and actually lifted their glasses to toast the spectacular scene. Their blithe attitude suddenly changed when water began pounding at the windows; they fled out a rear exit and reached high ground only moments before the flood broke in, wrecking the place.

Incredibly, Brush Creek's rampage actually seemed to draw excitement seekers to the scene. At one point a police sergeant reported to his dispatcher that an unruly crowd of 1,500 onlookers had gathered and that rescue work was being hindered by people climbing onto police cars to get a better look.

Such folly inevitably exacted a high price all over the area. Police later concluded that one 19-year-old youth had drowned when he drove too close to the edge of a rising stream; his car stalled and he was swiftly swallowed by the flood. Similarly, after the body of a 14-year-old boy was recovered from a swollen creek, his mother offered mournful explanation: "When it rained, if he saw a puddle, he'd walk through it. He liked to play in water."

Three months after Brush Creek had once more dwindled to a trickle within its concrete bed, the Weather Service issued a report on the disaster. Satellite

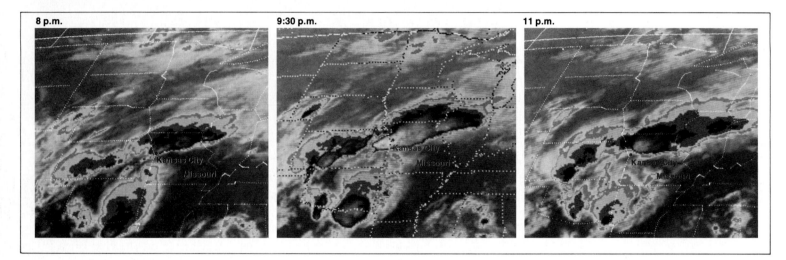

8 p.m.　　9:30 p.m.　　11 p.m.

data, it said, had been helpful in identifying the area of potential thunderstorms. Radar had been of "inestimable value." The forecasters' interpretation of the information at their disposal had been "very professional and competent." After the first flash-flood watch had been announced, "follow-up warnings were very good."

Yet the report concluded that many persons "did not accept the reality of the situation"—a somber understatement that might well serve as epitaph for the 25 victims of the Kansas City flash flood.

These infrared satellite images trace the thunderstorm that flooded Kansas City on September 12, 1977. At 8 p.m. *(far left),* a mass of warm, unstable cloud cover shows up as a dark blotch over northern Missouri. By 9:30 *(middle),* a large area of white shows up in the dark cloud image, indicating the cooling associated with a torrential downpour. By 11 *(above),* the area of white has decreased as the thunderstorm dissipates and moves off.

Despite such frustrations, the Weather Service has continued to plug steadily away at expanding its precipitation and stream-stage reporting network and at refining its instruments. Progress is painfully slow; dramatic breakthroughs are not expected. Yet flash-flood forecasters can point with increasing frequency to instances where their efforts have saved lives. As often as not, the successes are due at least as much to the human judgments of the forecasters as to the technological proficiency of their equipment.

On the evening of April 9, 1980, hydrologist David Curtis, whose specialty was flash floods, dropped by the Northeast River Forecasting Center in Bloomfield, Connecticut. Curtis was off duty, and he planned to spend a few hours working on his doctoral dissertation in water resources. He chatted for a while with the forecaster on duty, Bruce Whyte, then busied himself with his thesis.

The regular 7 p.m. forecast had called for light showers. But at about 10 o'clock Curtis learned of heavy rainfall outside in the same manner that most people do—he heard the water beating against the office windows. The downpour was so torrential that Curtis was immediately alerted to the threat of flash flooding in low-lying areas. Putting aside his thesis, Curtis went to work. "From then on," he recalls, "things got pretty hot and heavy."

As a first order of business, Curtis began dialing the numbers of rain gauges connected to the forecasting center by telephone circuitry. It was almost immediately apparent that a heavy storm had escaped the satellite and radar analysts. Based on the gauge reports, the storm extended across central and southwestern Connecticut. Greater Hartford had recorded 1.3 inches of rain, Wallingford .9 and Saugatuck 1.7. Adding to the evidence of a potentially troublesome situation, a cooperating New Haven television station with its own meteorological resources called to report thunderstorms in that area with rain falling at a rate of about one inch per hour.

At 10:30, Curtis called the Weather Service forecast office in Boston to discuss the worsening weather. Based on its most recent satellite imagery, Boston advised that the rains would soon ease. At 10:35, however, Curtis' concern was increased by two simultaneous events: The official in charge of flood control for the city of Hartford anxiously reported that streams in his area were approaching danger levels—and an automated gauge in a small stream in West Hartford set off an alarm buzzer in a local police station, indicating that flooding was already in progress. Recalls Curtis: "Now we were getting excited."

Quickly checking more gauges, Curtis and Whyte found that the heaviest concentrations of rain seemed to be along the north-south line of the lower Housatonic River, where a series of hydroelectric dams controls the flow of water. The gauge of the dam at Bull's Bridge recorded 1.76 inches, Rocky Run measured 2.02 and Falls Village 1.2. At Stevenson, site of the southernmost dam, 3.26 inches of rain had fallen.

With this worrisome information in hand, Curtis called the Weather Service office at Bridgeport, which had responsibility for the lower Housatonic zone, and suggested that a flash-flood warning be issued. "Bridgeport resisted," Curtis recalls. "Their radar readings indicated that the rain was nearly over. We disagreed. We thought we already had enough evidence and we felt strongly that the warning should go out."

Weather Service procedures generally assume that the forecasters nearest the scene of possible floods are in a better position to make decisions than those at more distant stations. Says Curtis: "What may be obvious to someone looking out a window may not be so obvious to a forecaster located many miles away." Nevertheless, although they had the authority to issue a warning, Whyte and Curtis deferred to Bridgeport.

In the cool, clinical confines of the Bloomfield office, with its powder-blue and lemon-yellow trim, its clicking teleprinters and its flashing computer screens, Curtis and Whyte worked side by side for nearly half an hour, rechecking their gauges. Not only was the rain continuing, but streams, including the wide Housatonic River, were approaching or exceeding flash-flood guidelines. These guidelines state that when streams receive more than 2.5 to three inches of rain within a three-hour period, flooding will occur.

"By then we *knew* we had enough," says Curtis. "We called Bridgeport and presented them with additional evidence and again advised them to put out a warning." This time Bridgeport agreed and immediately issued the warning. It was 11:45 p.m.

By midnight, flash floods were raging throughout western Connecticut and the Housatonic was out of its banks in several places. Local authorities, by then alerted, had begun to evacuate residents of low-lying neighborhoods in such cities and towns as Bridgeport, Fairfield, Derby and Stratford. And although damage to property was estimated at more than three million dollars, only one person—a 55-year-old woman whose car had stalled in the water of a flooding lake in Bridgeport—drowned on the night of April 9.

At dawn the Housatonic crested and began to return to its banks, as predicted. By then David Curtis, his job done, was at home, asleep. Ω

Steady rain, the legacy of a dying hurricane, had pelted Putnam, Connecticut, and the rest of New England for an entire day and night. Almost eight inches registered on the rain gauges—to be added to the four inches of rain dumped by a similar storm just the week before.

By the morning of August 19, 1955, this burden of water proved too great for a series of old stone-and-earth dams on the Quinebaug River 20 to 50 miles north of Putnam. One after another the dams gave way, and a torrent of water roared down the riverbed, reaching speeds downstream of 25 miles an hour, and leaping the banks in waves five feet high. The frenzied waters swept away bridges and roads, carved up railroad embankments, and damaged one quarter of the buildings and homes in the small manufacturing town of 8,200 people.

In the midst of the deluge, terrifying explosions rent the air. Water had poured into a warehouse stocked with 20 tons of magnesium, a chemical that ignites on contact with water. The warehouse erupted in flame, and hundreds of barrels of burning magnesium were carried downstream in the churning river. Firemen could only watch helplessly throughout the night as the barrels exploded, each blast lighting up Putnam like a giant flash bulb. Flames rose to a height of 250 feet, and smoke from the blazes could be seen 20 miles away.

Despite the wild scenes pictured at left and on the following pages, not one Putnam resident was lost to the flood. Throughout the storm, state police and civil-defense teams had kept watch on the dams and the river. An alert was sounded as the water rose in reservoirs behind the dams. Evacuation commenced by car, truck and bus, at radioed word of the first break. Some laggard residents were taken to safety by boat, and a few were plucked from rooftops by a National Guard helicopter.

A week later, after the waters had receded, the residents returned to their homes to begin the cleanup. What the rampant river had destroyed or damaged was reckoned at $13 million. It would take the people of Putnam months, and in some cases years, to rebuild. But thanks to prudent civil-defense measures, they were at least all alive.

A towering wall of water engulfs a bridge and washes down a street in Putnam, Connecticut, during the disastrous flood of August 19, 1955. The Quinebaug River, swollen by days of rain, was transformed into a furious torrent when a series of old and inadequate dams burst upstream.

Floodwaters swirl around a fire hydrant and debris lies piled against stores in Putnam's shopping district several hours after the crest of the Quinebaug passed through. In some parts of town, businesses were buried under 14 feet of rocks and silt.

Fire smolders in the ruins of a 100-year-old fieldstone mill on the banks of the Quinebaug where tons of explosive magnesium had been stored. The floodwaters triggered the conflagration by inducing a violent chemical reaction, and then prevented fire fighters from getting to the scene.

Main Street comes to an abrupt end where the tumultuous waves of the Quinebaug have torn away a concrete bridge. Three bridges crossed the river in Putnam; within a few hours, the flood destroyed them all, isolating one side of town from the other.

Putnam millworker and Red Cross volunteer
Howard Keach examines his own ruined furnishings,
after the flood reached the high-water mark visible
on the walls. "The Red Cross helped replace necessary
things like beds and furniture," recalled Doris
Keach. "But some things can't be replaced, like high
school yearbooks and pictures of the children."

A chair sits forlornly in the middle of a street and
autos lie half-buried in muck as the floodwaters
recede. To add to their problems, returning residents
found sewage backed up in their homes; to guard
against typhoid, the entire population was vaccinated.

Cleanup gets under way along railroad tracks twisted and broken by the force of the flood. Beyond repair, however, is part of the Putnam Technical School, which collapsed when the turbulent waters washed away the foundation of the building.

Chapter 5

"RUN! RUN! THE DAM IS BREAKING!"

Begun in 1785 during the reign of Spain's despotic Charles III and completed in 1791 under his son Charles IV, the spectacular structure on the Guadalentín River was considered the crowning achievement of Spanish dam builders, for 200 years the world's preeminent hydraulic engineers. Among other things, the Puentes Dam was by substantial measure the biggest such edifice erected anywhere up to that time. It stood 164 feet high and stretched 925 feet across the turbulent river in Murcia Province in the southeastern part of the country. At its crest it was 36 feet thick, widening to 145 feet at its base. The core consisted of rubble masonry set in mortar, and the facings on both sides were made of huge stones carefully cut and closely fitted.

In its design, Puentes was of the common gravity type, kept in place by its own great weight, with the pressure of the water behind the barrier being transferred by vertical compressive forces to the foundation of the dam. Puentes was, in short, built to give service for centuries. Yet it lasted scarcely 11 years—and in its failure it earned dubious renown as the first modern high dam to succumb to the fantastic pressures that all dams must endure.

It was, in fact, a wonder that the Puentes Dam survived for even 11 years. In the early stages of its construction, the engineers had discovered that the Guadalentín's hard-rock bed, which would form the dam's foundation, was split crosswise by a deep pocket of loose alluvial material—gravel and soil. Unless something radical was done, the dam would be rooted in earth too soft to bear its weight.

The Spanish engineers were undaunted. With all the ingenuity and skill that had made them the masters of their profession, they drove hundreds of timbers, each 20 feet long and about two feet square, into the alluvium. This forest of pilings was then braced at the top with horizontal timbers so as to form a grillwork, into which the masonry base of the dam was sunk to a depth of seven feet. Moreover, to prevent erosion caused by water spewing from the dam's sluiceway, the grille was extended 130 feet downstream, then covered with seven feet of masonry on which protective planking was placed.

Because of the stupendous weights and hydrostatic pressures involved, the process of impounding water in a reservoir is always critical in the life of a dam. But southeastern Spain is for the most part a parched land, and the demands of the population for water were such that for more than a decade the level of the Puentes reservoir was held to a maximum of 82 feet—less than 50 per cent of its capacity and hardly a stern test of the durability of the dam. Early in 1802, however, unusually heavy rain came to the region, the reservoir filled to a depth of 154 feet, a mere 10 feet from the top—and disaster struck.

Rude crosses stacked in front of coffins bear witness to the 2,600 victims of a particularly murderous and totally unanticipated flood in Italy's Piave valley in 1963. A great landslide dropped more than 300 million cubic yards of rock into the Vaiont reservoir, sending a 330-foot-high wave of water cascading over the top of a dam and onto the sleeping villages below.

Francisco Oliver, one of the few eyewitnesses who survived, left a written account of the terrible event: "About half past two on the afternoon of 30 April 1802, it was noticed that on the downstream side of the dam, toward the apron, water of a very red color was bubbling out and spreading in the shape of a palm tree." Continued Oliver, "About three o'clock, there was an explosion in the discharge-wells," two holes that were built into the dam to carry off excess water. "At the same time," he wrote, "the water escaping at the downstream side increased in volume. In a short time a second explosion was heard and, enveloped by an enormous mass of water, the piles, beams and other pieces of wood that formed the pile-work of the foundation and of the apron were forced upward.

"Immediately afterward a new explosion occurred, and the two big gates that closed the sluiceway or scouring-gallery, a tunnel intended to remove silt from the reservoir, fell in"—as did its central supporting pier. "At the same instant," Oliver wrote, "a mountain of water escaped in the form of an arc; it looked frightful and had a red color, caused either by the mud with which it was charged, or by the reflection of the sun."

At the first signs of trouble a messenger had been sent running to the town of Lorca, 12 miles downstream, to inform the director of the dam, Don Antonio Robles Vives. Down the valley behind him now came an estimated two billion gallons of water. The messenger took to the hills and escaped. As for the unfortunate Don Antonio Robles Vives, he drowned—along with 607 others.

The destruction of the Puentes Dam was, lamentably, by no means a singular event. Dams are the bulkiest structures made by man—and potentially the most dangerous. Among their blessings they bestow flood control, electric power, irrigation, ample supplies of water for human and industrial consumption, and even recreational facilities. Among their banes they bring death and ruin. Said John Smeaton, dean of 18th Century Britain's civil engineers: "There is not a more difficult or hazardous piece of work within the compass of civil engineering than the establishment of a high dam upon a rapid river that is liable to great and sudden floods."

By rough estimate, there are more than 50,000 dams in the world that stand 50 feet or higher; close to 40 rise to 600 feet or more, and the highest are around 1,000 feet. Each and every one of these high dams represents a potential flood peril. Since the 12th Century A.D. an estimated 2,000 dams have suffered failures, and during the 20th Century alone more than 8,000 persons have perished in more than 200 major dam breaks—a rate of about three breaks a year.

To the engineers responsible for designing and erecting safe dams, such statistics represent an appalling reality. Robert B. Jansen, a former member of the International Commission on Large Dams, recently wrote: "Dams require defensive engineering, which means listing every imaginable force that might be imposed, examination of every possible set of circumstances, and incorporation of protective elements to cope with each and every condition."

That task is almost impossible to accomplish, if only because the number of things that can go wrong with a dam is virtually without limit. Still, some broad categories can be established. For example, a 1962 Spanish study of 308 major dam breaks found that foundation failure was the cause in 40 per cent of the cases. Inadequate spillway capacity was the culprit in 23 per cent of the breaks, while poor construction, uneven settlement and various other problems were the causes in the remaining 37 per cent.

Foundations are a bugaboo. "No structure grips the ground so closely as a dam," said French engineer André Coyne in 1939. "It holds on at its base and its flanks. In other words, a dam is made up of two parts: the artificial dam, man-made, and the natural dam that continues it, surrounds it and

An earth dam is built of compacted soil and sand shaped into a triangular embankment on top of a watertight clay core. The upstream face is often covered with rock to prevent erosion from waves.

A rockfill dam is filled with assorted loose rock and, like the earth dam, is triangular in shape. The upstream side is covered with tight-fitting concrete or asphalt to keep water from penetrating the loose rock.

A gravity dam is made of giant concrete blocks or stones sealed with grout or liquid cement. By the laws of physics, the force of the water in the reservoir is deflected downward, helping to anchor the dam.

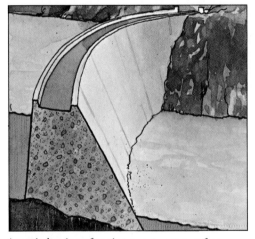

An arch dam has a face that curves upstream from bank to bank. The compressive strength of the arch transmits water pressure to the side abutments and foundation, bonding the dam to the canyon.

Triangular supports on the downstream side of a buttress dam strengthen it and help distribute water pressure to the foundation. The watertight upstream face is inclined at an angle of about 45 degrees.

Dams of various sorts have been built to control the flow of rivers since the earliest days of civilization. But it was not until the 1800s and the advent of sophisticated hydraulic and structural engineering that dam building evolved into a modern science.

Today, there are five principal types of dams in use around the world, constructed from three basic materials: earth, rock and concrete. Which type of dam is chosen for a particular river depends on the geology, topography and climate of the region.

In general, earth and rockfill dams are the most feasible types for rivers that run through broad valleys. It often takes an immense structure to contain such a river, and earth and rock are the most economical materials available. Earth dams are the commonest. With broad bases that distribute weight over a wide area, they are the only dams that can be built on a soft, unstable riverbed. Eight out of every 10 dams in the United States, Canada and the Soviet Union are earth dams. Where rock is plentiful, rockfill dams are equally effective. But their heavier weight requires a solid foundation.

Dams built primarily of concrete are found in narrow valleys with hard bedrock to anchor and support them. There are three kinds of concrete dams. Gravity dams use their great bulk and weight to resist water pressure. These huge dams—which include Washington State's Grand Coulee Dam, with its fantastic 10.6 million cubic yards of concrete—are strong enough to hold up even when floodwaters overtop their crests. But they are costly. Arch dams, the second kind, are more economical because they rely on the physics of their curved shape to bear the stress load rather than on their sheer weight. But during a flood, a small break in an arch dam can swiftly lead to total failure.

A happy medium is the buttress dam, which relies on both weight and structural elements. The weight of the water on the dam's sharply inclined face actually adds to its stability through the force and counterforce of the buttresses; the strength of the buttresses also helps the dam withstand minor foundation movements—making it the engineer's choice for seismically active areas.

on which it is founded. The more important of the two is the latter, which is unnoticed."

For many centuries, dam builders fretted far more about the shapes, the dimensions and the materials that went into their dams than they did about the geology that supported the structures. Indeed, it was well into the 20th Century before the first systematic experiments were made in rock mechanics—the behavior of rock under stress and heavy loads—a science even yet in its infancy.

Solid, unweathered rock such as granite makes an ideal foundation material. But it is rarely present in sufficient quantities at the places where the builders, guided by a host of other considerations, wish to erect their dams. Instead, the engineers must often make do with flawed foundation substances of seemingly infinite variety. Faults, fissures and clay veins in granite are obvious sources of weakness. Sand, gravel and other loose materials in joints and cracks are vulnerable to the phenomenon known as piping, which occurs when the pressure of water from seepage simply washes the soil particles away, leaving conduits that enlarge themselves and undermine the dam. Similarly, a dam may collapse because of the large cavities that are left when such sedimentary rocks as limestone are dissolved by percolating water.

Slates, schists and sedimentary shales have thin, flat, laminated planes; when subjected to load, the layers can slide like a deck of cards, carrying all or part of a dam downstream. Even the firmest rock formations are compressed and deformed under the weight of a dam and its reservoir. As a result, all dams settle to some degree. If the settling is uniform, there is little need for concern, but if it is uneven because of irregularities or variations in the underlying geology, the dam may be fatally damaged.

To be sure, certain remedial measures can be taken against most such geological debilities. Extensive instrumentation of many dams now enables engineers to identify weak spots. Fissures can be filled with grout, a thin mixture of liquid cement, injected under high pressure. Rock masses can be bolted together. To lock a dam into place and to make the foundation more watertight, a cutoff trench, into which the massive structure is built, is sometimes excavated to a depth of 100 or more feet.

Yet despite the efficacy of such engineering techniques, the specialized knowledge of the geologist is critical to the selection of a safe site. And the engineer who barges ahead largely on his own, either without full and complete geological advice or ignoring it, can cause untold sorrow—as the residents of California's fecund Santa Clara Valley learned in 1928.

In what was to prove a fateful moment for California, a strapping, dirt-poor Irish immigrant named William Mulholland, then 22, set foot on the wharf at San Pedro one day in 1877. Mulholland soon made his way to the sleepy, sunbaked town of Los Angeles, whose inhabitants still got their scanty supplies of water from open trenches fed by the Los Angeles River. What Los Angeles, otherwise generously endowed by nature, desperately needed to transform it into a great city was more water—and Mulholland was just the man to provide that precious commodity.

With little previous schooling, Mulholland educated himself as an engineer, and by 1902 he had become chief engineer and general manager of the crucially important Los Angeles Bureau of Water Works and Supply. He was a dominating, even domineering, man of empirical judgments and grand dreams. He devised a method for transporting water to the Los Angeles area through a system of aqueducts and for storing it in a network of reservoirs. In recognition both of his personality and of his achievements, he was known, quite simply, as "the Chief."

Mulholland's masterpiece was a 233-mile aqueduct, including 52 miles of tunnels that he blasted and bored through hard rock along the eastern side of

William Mulholland, chief engineer of the Los Angeles water department, stands with his surveyor's level on a hillside near the city. Although he was an excellent and careful engineer, Mulholland ignored some obvious geological problems when he chose the site of the St. Francis Dam in 1924—an error that was to prove fatal four years later.

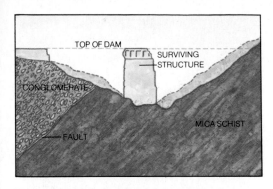

The unstable geological formations that caused California's St. Francis Dam to collapse in 1928 are shown in cross section. The northwestern abutment was rooted in an amalgam of pebbles, clay and gypsum, likely to give way under pressure or when saturated. The southeastern abutment rested on mica schist, which is subject to slippage. Both ends of the dam broke free, loosing 12.4 billion gallons of water into the canyon below.

the rugged Sierra Nevada. At one point, 45 miles north of Los Angeles, the aqueduct emerged from a five-mile-long tunnel and dropped precipitously into the San Francisquito Canyon, a pass leading into the Santa Clara Valley. Mulholland decided to use the energy of the water as it plunged 1,000 feet within the aqueduct as a source of hydroelectric power, and to that end he constructed two concrete power stations. Shortly after, he decided to build a dam across the canyon midway between the two power stations. Its reservoir, supplied by the aqueduct's surpluses, would store enough water to last Los Angeles for one year in case of emergency.

Unfortunately, the headstrong Chief, himself an amateur geologist, was not much of a man for seeking advice, least of all from those professionals who might have warned him off. He therefore constructed his new St. Francis Dam without any consultation whatever—despite the fact that the canyon's floor was a geological nightmare.

On the northwestern side of the canyon were thick deposits of conglomerate, ranging in size from fine silts and stones, some greater than eight inches in diameter, to clay and highly soluble gypsum. Even the simplest tests would have shown that the dry conglomerate crushed when placed under a weight of 500 pounds per square inch, or 36 tons per square foot—far less than the burden Mulholland proposed to place upon it. Moreover, in a dramatic demonstration made long after the St. Francis Dam had been destroyed, a fist-sized chunk of the conglomerate was placed in a glass container of water. In the words of a laboratory report, "a startling change takes place. Absorption proceeds rapidly, air bubbles are given off, flakes and particles begin to fall, and the water becomes turbid with suspended clay. After 15 minutes to an hour the rock has disintegrated into a deposit of loose sand and small fragments covered by muddy water."

The southeastern side and the canyon floor were geologically almost as horrifying. They were composed of fragile mica schist, which had a distressing tendency to break into thin, flat, slatelike pieces; the schist was interspersed with talc, making it slippery and especially subject to sliding.

To cap it all, the two grossly diverse rock formations were split by a geologic fault. Although it was classified as "dead," meaning that the land on either side had not to anyone's knowledge moved in a very long while, the faces were striped with serpentine—a hydrous magnesium silicate—which, when softened by water, could be gouged out by hand.

Engineer Mulholland chose to ignore this treacherous footing; his vision was too grand to be questioned. He proceeded apace to build his dam—and a splendid one it was. Like Spain's Puentes Dam, it was of the gravity type and depended on its own weight to keep it in place. In addition, Mulholland employed an arched shape, which added strength to the dam. Mulholland's great edifice required 137,000 cubic yards of concrete; when completed in 1926 the St. Francis Dam stood 205 feet high, spanned 700 feet and was 175 feet thick at its base, tapering to a crest width of 16 feet with a low wing wall extension of 588 feet. Impounded in the reservoir behind the dam was 38,000 acre-feet of water.

Almost from the beginning the dam leaked and showed cracks. But the Chief remained unperturbed. After all, he correctly noted, every dam experiences a certain amount of seepage and concrete dams always crack a little. Despite the fact that he had done no grouting in the foundation rock, Mulholland insisted that the St. Francis was "the driest dam of its size I ever saw."

For nearly two years the giant concrete mass stood resolutely across the San Francisquito Canyon. Water dribbled continuously from its base and at its western abutment. Then, on the morning of March 12, 1928, damkeeper Tony Harnischfeger, while making his rounds, spotted a new leak on the west, or conglomerate, side. He called Mulholland in Los Angeles and the Chief sped to the scene in his chauffeured limousine, arriving at about 10:30 a.m. An inspection showed that the seeping water was clear, indicating that it was not eroding the foundation soil. Satisfied that there was no imminent danger, Mulholland drove back to the city in time for a late lunch.

At 11:47 p.m. an employee at Powerplant No. 1, five miles above the dam, routinely put in a telephone call to Powerplant No. 2, one and a half miles below the barrier. Nothing unusual was reported. Ten minutes later, at exactly 11:57:30, the lights in Los Angeles briefly flickered. On a hill above Powerplant No. 2, a house began shuddering, windows rattled—and the lights went out. Monitoring instruments showed that a transmission line in the canyon was broken at 11:58. By then, some 12 billion gallons of water were speeding toward the Santa Clara Valley nine miles away.

Down the gorge, an employee of the power company was awakened in his home by a tremendous roar. Rushing outside, he saw a 120-foot wave bearing down on him; he spotted the roof of a building being tossed about in the wild water, somehow climbed aboard and was finally dumped—alive—at a high place on the canyon's wall. In a construction camp, 150 men were asleep in their tents; only 66 survived, having miraculously managed to ride the wave to safety.

On California Highway No. 126 in the Santa Clara Valley, the traffic was light, thanks to the lateness of the hour. Even so, it has been estimated that some 50 automobiles, carrying as many as 125 persons, were swept away by the

A photograph of Southern California's St. Francis Dam taken shortly after its completion in 1926 shows the dam wedged snugly between rock abutments that later proved to be disastrously unstable. The discoloration in the middle of the dam's concrete face was caused by water from the reservoir's outlet gate.

floodwaters. Some of these vehicles were later found buried in mud more than 20 miles from the roadway. As the torrent moved across the broad valley, it slowed and spread into a two-mile-wide stream of sullen, debris-laden water before finally pouring into the Pacific Ocean, 44 miles from the mouth of the San Francisquito Canyon.

Inspection of the damsite the next morning showed that a section of the dam weighing as much as 3,000 tons had been carried a half mile down the canyon. Another section almost as large had been overturned.

The inquiries into the causes of the St. Francis Dam disaster were long, bitter, confusing—and perhaps academic. In fact, the dam might easily have been doomed by any one of the three flawed elements in its foundation: the conglomerate, the schist or the fault. An official report finally concluded that the collapse of the St. Francis Dam could be attributed "wholly to the unsuitability of the materials on which the dam was built."

A Los Angeles coroner's jury, conducting an inquest, also said pointedly that "the construction and operation of a great dam should never be left to the sole judgment of one man, no matter how eminent." As for 73-year-old William Mulholland, he bore the burden of his mistakes like the man that he was. "Don't blame anybody else," he said; "you just fasten it on me. If there was an error of human judgment, I was the human."

That was of no comfort to the estimated 420 other humans who died in the St. Francis flood.

Perhaps because it was such a blatant instance of perilous site selection, raising few if any questions that could not have been answered beforehand, the St. Francis tragedy did little to spur further research into the geological causes of dam failures. Conversely, the 1959 catastrophe that overtook an arch—as opposed to a gravity—dam on the French Riviera did inspire studies that not only solved the mystery of the structure's collapse but significantly added to the sum of knowledge about rock mechanics.

"An arch dam is a kind of bridge overturned in an upstream direction," said France's André Coyne, who specialized in designing the type. "The oldest

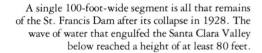

A single 100-foot-wide segment is all that remains of the St. Francis Dam after its collapse in 1928. The wave of water that engulfed the Santa Clara Valley below reached a height of at least 80 feet.

known examples are just like this, and if the comparison seems a bit far-fetched today it is because we vary the thicknesses and curvature so as to try and adjust our arches to the shapes of the valleys and thrust of the water."

Developed in the 17th Century but infrequently built until the 20th, when it bloomed in the form of tall, slender dams of remarkable strength and surpassing elegance, the arch type derives its stability not from its bulk but from its shape. Using the classic arch principle, in which load pressure, called thrust, is transmitted outward and laterally from one section to another, the arch dam depends less on the strength of its foundation than on the strength of the natural rock abutments at either end. The greater the thrust of water

131

against it, the tighter the dam is pressed against the abutments and the stronger it becomes—for as long as the abutments hold. Furthermore, because the weight of an arch dam has little relevance to its stability, it requires less construction material than any other type of dam; reduced costs are a happy by-product of the design.

The design of arch dams obviously demands that they abut against sound walls of solid, unyielding rock. In that sense the Malpasset Dam, in the narrow valley of France's Reyran River near the small Riviera town of Fréjus, seemed to be ideally situated. And thus the dam's demise was caused by neither the rock abutments nor the arch principle—but rather, for reasons beyond the day's scientific ken, by the old nemesis of foundation failure.

Malpasset was a thing of concrete grace, the world's thinnest arch dam, no more than 22 feet thick at any point from its base to its 217-foot crest as it arced in a 732-foot curve between its rock abutments. Work on the structure began in the spring of 1952, and on April 20, 1954, the four-mile-long reservoir was ready for filling.

For five years the level of the reservoir increased gradually, keeping pace with the demand for water, but never straining its capacity or nearing the crest of the dam. Beginning in mid-November, 1959, however, intermittent but heavy rainfall drenched the area, causing the water in the reservoir to rise by six feet until, at noon on December 2, it stood no more than eight feet below the top of the dam. By 6 o'clock that evening it had crept up another six inches, and the outlet valve was opened in order to let some of the water escape. The rise ceased and, ever so slowly, the level receded. By 7:30 p.m. it had dropped just over one inch.

The keeper, his day's work done, left the dam at 8:45 p.m. and retired to his home on a hill about a mile downstream. His repose was violently interrupted. At about 9:10 he heard a series of explosive sounds. These were followed by a concussive gust of wind that blew open his doors and shattered the windows. After a brilliant flash in the night, the lights went out—the power line from the dam broke at 9:13.

The flood that was unleashed by the breakup of the Malpasset Dam demolished Fréjus, five miles downstream, killing 421 people on its seven-mile run to the Mediterranean.

But though the fact of the disaster was all too stark, its cause remained cloaked in doubt. For months a commission appointed by the French Ministry of Agriculture examined the possibilities and in August 1960 filed a 55-page report supported by three bulky volumes containing 40 annexes. It found no fault with the dam's design and noted that the stress calculations had been accurate and that both the construction work and the quality of the concrete were good. The chance that the dam had buckled because of an earthquake was investigated, but no unusual seismic activity had been reported. The commission looked for evidence of sabotage but found nothing. The remote possibility that the dam had been hit by a meteorite was briefly considered and swiftly discarded.

Even though an arch dam places much more stress on its abutments than on its foundation, suspicion centered on the bedrock beneath the structure. It was composed of gneiss—a banded rock that was considered first-rate foundation material—with dense, irregular microfissures. On-site inspection disclosed the hitherto undiscovered presence of a small fault in the gneiss that cropped out about 100 feet downstream from the dam, then angled at 45 degrees and passed upstream about 50 feet beneath the barrier's base. But even if the designers had known about the flaw they would probably have remained undisturbed, since the dam's horizontal stresses should not have caused movement along the fault below.

Still, a culprit was needed—and the commission finally settled on one. Since

The Tiny Cracks
That Doomed a Dam

The year was 1976, and the United States Bureau of Reclamation's engineers in charge of the construction of Idaho's Teton Dam were well satisfied with their creation.

Many of the techniques were state of the art. The 307-foot-high earthfill dam on the Teton River was protected from undermining by a complex of deep trenches filled with compacted soil and capped with concrete. As added security beneath the trenches, the engineers installed a thick curtain of concrete 3,000 feet long and 260 feet deep in spots. Moreover, special outlet works were included in the design to prevent too-rapid filling of the reservoir.

But errors, both of omission and of commission, marred the dam. A "tight seal," according to regulations, demanded only that cracks wider than a half inch be grouted with concrete; lesser "joints," as the cracks were called, could be ignored. Further, although the lake behind the dam had been filling since October 1975, the outlet works needed to maintain a moderate fill pace were still unfinished the following June.

As it turned out, the dam was afflicted with myriad small cracks, and these, combined with the swiftly rising water pressure, spelled disaster. In the seam between the trench system and the curtain of concrete, water ate into the cracks in the earthfill and scoured them out to produce pipelike holes in the dam.

On June 5, a muddy trickle observed in early morning on the downstream embankment grew to a steady flow within a few hours as the piping widened to a tunnel. A vain effort to plug the leak brought bulldozers to the scene at 11:30 a.m. But within half an hour the roof of the tunnel disintegrated in an onrush of water and mud, and the dam was gone.

By the day's end, 11 people were dead and 25,000 homeless in riverside towns in the path of the flood.

In a remarkable sequence, photographer Dale Howard captured the disastrous 1976 collapse of Idaho's Teton Dam. At top, a bulldozer tries to fill in the first gaps in the dam face, but the roof of a tunnel caused by erosion soon caves in. In the middle photo, an avalanche of rock breaks loose and buries the dozer minutes after its driver had fled. In the final photo, the crest of the dam collapses, and a turquoise torrent scours a wide path for the Teton River.

no blame could be ascribed to the dam or its construction, the overloading of the reservoir, the commission concluded, had caused the western abutment and the underlying rock to move.

That answer satisfied hardly anyone, and other geologists and engineers soon began chipping in with their own ideas, which were as confusing as they were diverse. Nonetheless, there was general agreement that the solution to the riddle of Malpasset had something to do with the behavior of rock under pressure and strain. That gave rise to a greatly increased interest in the neglected science of rock mechanics, on which only a few books and papers had previously been published.

Therein lay the secret. Within a decade of the disaster, French researchers were conducting experiments into how stress affects the permeability of various rock types. They found that rocks with many microfissures, such as the Malpasset gneiss, lost permeability to about $1/100$ of their normal condition when placed under heavy pressure. On the other hand, when placed under tension, or stretched during seepage of water into its pores, the gneiss exhibited a permeability far above normal.

At Malpasset, the overloading of the reservoir had forced water into just such an area of tension at the end of the reservoir behind the dam; as the water tried to escape, it was blocked by the compressed, and therefore virtually watertight, gneiss beneath the foundation. Intolerable upward pressure accumulated—and finally blasted out the rock from underneath the dam. As the footing exploded, the beautiful dam was destroyed.

As if such secret geologic forces lurking beneath and on the flanks of dams were not trouble enough, the rock formations beneath and around reservoirs must also be considered a potential source of trouble.

Dams exist for a variety of purposes that make different—and often conflicting—demands on their reservoirs. For example, the reservoir of a dam erected solely for flood control should, ideally, be kept at low levels so as to save space for floodwater storage. At the opposite extreme, the reservoir of a hydroelectric dam should be kept as full as possible to maintain water pressure. When, as frequently happens, a reservoir is meant to fulfill both functions, it is up to the hydrologists and engineers who control its level to strike the precarious balance between needs and safety. Such was the dilemma confronting the operators of Italy's Vaiont Dam.

High in the Alps of northeastern Italy, the Vaiont River has slashed a deep, narrow gorge between limestone walls. There, about a mile above the point where the Vaiont joins the Piave River and enters a broad valley, what was then the world's highest—860 feet—arch dam was completed in the autumn of 1960. The major purpose of the Vaiont Dam was to provide hydroelectric power; flood control was a secondary consideration.

Stretching from the west to the east behind the dam was a reservoir with a planned capacity of 137,000 acre-feet of water. Immediately to its south loomed Mount Toc, on whose northern slope, overlooking the lake, the remains of a prehistoric rockslide covered an area of about one square mile. Composed mainly of limestone, with layers of weak, crumbly marl, the mass was fundamentally unstable. But most engineers and geologists reckoned that although relatively small slides would probably occur, the bulk of the steeply sloped upper mass would eventually be stabilized by the more gently sloped lower beds.

Nevertheless, the engineers determined to keep a close eye on the frowning face of Mount Toc, and even as water began to fill the reservoir in 1960 they placed markers on the slope so as to measure its movement. They soon discovered that whenever the level of the reservoir rose, the mass on the mountain moved downslope. As the water level increased, so did the speed of rock

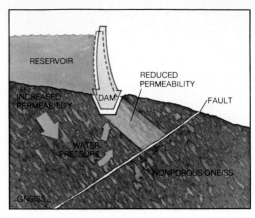

How water pressure unseated France's Malpasset Dam and caused it to fail in 1959 is shown above. Water entered microfissures in the gneiss rock beneath the reservoir and gradually built up immense pressure in the area at the base of the dam. When this water under pressure, seeking escape, encountered a zone of impermeable gneiss that had been compressed by the dam's weight, it was deflected sharply upward, lifting half the dam from its saddle in the steep gorge and leading to a blowout along its concrete face.

The Mystery of the Channeled Scablands

In 1923 a geologist by the name of J. Harlen Bretz, who had surveyed the dramatically ridged and pitted lavas of Washington State's Columbia Plateau, published a paper that contained a fantastic notion. Could these wild landforms have been sculpted by a catastrophic flood that had reshaped the entire face of eastern Washington? Bretz dubbed the desolate panorama the Channeled Scablands and wrote that they were "wounds only partially healed" from a great flood sometime during the last Ice Age.

At first, Bretz's theory was regarded as outrageous. But his field work and that of numerous other geologists over the next three decades proved him absolutely right —not only about Washington, but also about parts of neighboring Idaho and Montana. With glaciers covering much of North America 18,000 years ago, a 2,000-foot-high ice dam had formed in the Rockies, blocking the flow of Montana's Clark Fork River. An immense glacial lake had spread out across 3,000 square miles—and then, as the ice melted, had burst through the dam, hurling a wall of water, icebergs and debris west across the Idaho panhandle and down through Washington's lava field.

Geologist Bretz lived to see his theory vindicated and its scope expanded. In the space age, scientists speculate that such glacial-lake outbursts may offer clues to the vast erosion channels photographed by Viking spacecraft on Mars.

Giant ripple marks near Camas Hot Springs, Montana, bear witness to the irresistible currents that pounded gravel into mile-long ridges after an enormous glacial lake burst through its ice dam some 18,000 years ago. Geologists estimate that the water roared through Clark Fork Canyon at the rate of 2.8 billion gallons per second.

movement; when the water came to within 85 feet of the crest of the dam, the mass on the mountain slid downward at more than half an inch per day.

The hydroelectric demands made upon the dam and its reservoir were, however, heavy, and by April of 1963 the engineers had gingerly permitted the water to rise to 76 feet below the spillway atop the dam, having convinced themselves that the danger from the mountain would abate. "It was assumed," an engineering report later said, "that the mass would eventually reach a certain equilibrium, or at least would keep moving so slowly that no serious problems would occur."

Heavy summer rains swelled the reservoir to a height greater than ever before—only 41 feet below the crest of the dam. And the movement on the mountain increased to alarming proportions. The lake was quickly lowered, but this time inexorable forces had been set in motion, and the creep continued. More rains not only hampered lowering of the reservoir but also saturated the mountain's slope. Plainly, the accumulating groundwater was exerting an upward pressure and causing subsurface rock on the lower slope to weaken and shift.

Around the 1st of October, the animals accustomed to grazing on the slope of Mount Toc suddenly departed the pastures—they were evidently more sensitive than humans to the minuscule movements of the ground underneath them. On the 8th of October, the engineers finally realized that they were dealing with a shifting mass that covered an area five times larger than they had previously supposed. To relieve the reservoir and reduce the water table beneath the threatening mass, two outlet tunnels in the left abutment of the dam were opened, and water began pouring through at a rate of more than 37,000 gallons per second.

But it was too late. At 10:41:40 on the dark and rainy night of October 9, 1963, the side of Mount Toc slid into the Vaiont reservoir. In a titanic movement that registered on seismographs throughout central and western Europe, more than 314 million cubic yards of rock, traveling at speeds of up to 100 feet per second, crashed into the reservoir, filling the lower end of the lake and displacing a fantastic volume of water. Waves surged up both sides of the valley; one climbed an unbelievable 460 feet above the level of the reservoir. A violent updraft sucked sprays of both water and rock higher still against the opposite slope. There, more than 850 feet above the reservoir in the hillside village of Casso, one man jumped from his bed when he felt an air blast hit his home. As he reached the door, the roof, followed by a shower of rock and water, fell onto the vacated bed.

At the same instant a mountainous wave of water rose 330 feet above the Vaiont Dam—which, in testimony to the strength of its arch structure, remained standing—rolled over its top, and smashed down onto the canyon floor far below. About two minutes after the rockslide had begun, a 230-foot wall of water leveled the town of Longarone, a mile downstream from the dam at the confluence of the Vaiont and the Piave Rivers, killing nearly all the inhabitants. From there the flood spread over the Piave valley, swamping the villages of Pirago, Villanova and Rivalta. Then the water receded, leaving 2,600 corpses in its ebb.

It had all happened in less than 15 minutes.

Los Angeles' St. Francis, France's Malpasset and Italy's Vaiont were all well-designed, well-built dams. They met their doom because of underlying geologic weaknesses—vagaries of nature that their builders either failed or refused to recognize. But many other dams have collapsed with calamitous results because of flaws in the structures themselves: errant design, shoddy workmanship or faulty operation. Expert engineering is, of course, a paramount requirement, and in 1874, after a small private Massachusetts dam broke down because its builder had not troubled to consult professional engineers, one member of an investigating committee commented acidly: "I do not believe, however much we are an evolved species, that we are derived from beavers; a man cannot make a dam by instinct or intuition."

Yet as even the most abbreviated list of dam disasters amply illustrates, engineers are themselves prey to human error. Moreover, the best-laid engineering plans as they appear on the drawing board can be wasted in the hands of cost-cutting, headstrong or generally inefficient contractors.

Between 1878 and 1881, the builders of France's Bouzey Dam made mortar with lime and dirty sand instead of cement and clean sand—a fact that clearly contributed to the dam's failure in April of 1895, when some 100 lives were lost. In 1911, near Austin, Pennsylvania, 80 people died after a concrete grav-

A marvel of civil engineering, the Vaiont Dam in the Italian Alps rises 860 feet above the valley floor in a graceful arch design so inherently strong that the structure needed to be only 74 feet thick at the base and 11 feet thick at the top. But a geologic flaw undid everything in 1963 as millions of tons of rock and mud suddenly slid into the reservoir from the slope at right, shooting eight billion gallons of water over the top of the dam. Miraculously, the dam held, but a wide area downstream was devastated.

Chapter 6

WHEN THE DELUGE CEASED

As the African sun glared down upon the burning sand and granite wilderness at Aswan, 590 miles to the south of Cairo, the yacht *Ramses* slipped gracefully through the gap that had been deliberately left in a cofferdam on the Nile River. On the deck of the yacht were Egypt's President Gamal Abdel Nasser, Soviet Premier Nikita S. Khrushchev and, for reasons not readily apparent, Yemen's President Abdulla Al-Sallal, each clutching a rock inscribed with words befitting the momentous occasion. At a signal, the three leaders ceremoniously flung their rocks into the river; shortly thereafter they stepped onto the shore.

The men landed to a wild cacophony. Throngs of people who had gathered along both banks of the river cheered, klaxons blared and the engines of hundreds of 25-ton trucks roared. Moving six abreast, the first trucks backed up to the edges of the gap and unloaded their rock contents into the void below. The gap was soon plugged, and the waters of the Nile began to rise behind the cofferdam, whose task it was to hold the river at bay until the following day.

At half past nine on the following morning—May 14, 1964—the leaders, now joined by Iraq's President Abduf Salam Muhammad Arif, returned to the cofferdam. Awaiting them were 34,000 laborers who had toiled toward this moment for almost four and a half years. Within an enormous tented pavilion, the guests of honor sat through ceremonial speeches, which were rendered in both Arabic and Russian. Then Gamal Nasser, who had staked the future of Egypt on this project, and Nikita Khrushchev, whose Union of Soviet Socialist Republics had helped to finance it, moved to a nearby table and, together, pressed a button.

With a muffled explosion, sand showered from an embankment sealing the entrance to a diversion channel that had been slashed, 198 feet wide and 200 feet deep, through the solid granite on the river's east bank. Water began to trickle into the channel.

The trickle became a stream and then a torrent, swallowing at one gulp a man who had chosen to watch from an unfortunate vantage point. The water rushed through 1,148 yards of open channel, disappeared into the darkness of six 312-yard tunnels and emerged in another stretch of open sluiceway before returning to the old riverbed after a 2,000-yard detour.

In the riverbed area vacated by the diversion, work could now get under way on the monumental High Dam at Aswan—which, for better or worse, would forever change the relationship between Egypt and the great river that had, since the beginning of civilized time, been both benefactor and scourge.

A Muslim laborer pauses for evening prayer during construction of Egypt's great High Dam at Aswan on the Nile River. At this early stage of the project in 1964, an immense canal *(foreground)* has been hewn through solid granite to divert the waters of the Nile while work proceeds on the dam itself. Part of the canal consists of tunnels *(background)* that will eventually serve as intakes for the hydroelectric plant.

From its rise in the Ethiopian highlands, source of the Blue Nile, and the equatorial East African plateau, whence flows the White Nile, the world's longest (4,132 miles) river drains one tenth of the African continent from a basin of 1.2 million square miles that includes 10 countries: Burundi, Tanzania, Rwanda, Uganda, the Central African Republic, Zaire, Kenya, Sudan, Ethiopia and Egypt. In its adventurous progress from south to north the Nile River traverses snow-draped mountains, magnificent lakes, measureless swamps, jungles primeval and, finally, the largest, most pitiless expanse of desert existing upon the earth.

During its 950-mile course across the Egyptian Sahara and, from Cairo to the Mediterranean, through the rich delta of its own creation, the Nile receives the waters of not a single tributary. Along this stretch of the river runs the green ribbon of Egypt's only arable real estate, nowhere more than 15 miles wide except in the delta. The rest of the country is desert, bleak, hostile and virtually uninhabited. Thus, 97 per cent of Egypt's 42 million people live and work on only 2.5 per cent of the land. And for thousands of years the Egyptians had been utterly dependent for their survival upon the annual rise and fall of the Nile. As the Greek historian Herodotus wrote: "Egypt is the Nile and the Nile is Egypt."

Perhaps as long ago as 4000 B.C., humans who lived on the flood plain of the lower Nile established small primitive settlements on "tortoise backs" —natural gravel and sand escarpments—and began to till the land that the river had made rich. From that dim moment of prehistory until the building of the High Dam at Aswan, Egypt lay at the mercy of the seasonal weather patterns of the remote Ethiopian highlands, from which come 84 per cent of the Nile's waters.

For most of each year, Ethiopia's high plateau is relatively dry. But in June the rains begin to descend upon the rugged, steeply sloped region, reaching peak volume toward the end of July and diminishing gradually through August and September. During that period, as many as 60 inches of rain may fall, feeding and swelling the Blue Nile.

In Egypt the river begins to rise in late June or early July, usually cresting in September and slowly subsiding thereafter. Throughout history the annual volume of the Nile has fluctuated greatly, depending on how much rain falls on the highlands. In low-flood years the Nile has discharged as little as 12 trillion gallons of water; in years of massive torrent, the discharge has soared to nearly 40 trillion gallons.

The first Egyptians could only suffer the Nile's moods. But by the 20th Century B.C., according to Herodotus, knowledge of the river and determination to harness its cycles had reached a point where the 12th Dynasty Pharaoh Amenemhet III completed, at a site 60 miles southwest of Cairo, what was probably history's first substantial river-control project. This was an irrigation canal 300 feet wide and 10 miles long leading from the Nile to a natural depression in the land; a dam with sluice gates was built across the canal to allow floodwaters to pass into the depression and to impound them there until they were needed for crops during the dry season.

Whether or not the project succeeded has been lost to history. But it may well have been a disappointment, because for many centuries thereafter the Egyptians eschewed such works. Instead, they sought to make the great river work for them in a simple and direct fashion. The system that they evolved was based on the promise of an annual flood and was known as basin irrigation. The land along the river was divided into sections that ranged in size from 2,000 acres to 83,000 acres, and the sections were separated by embankments, or dikes.

The stages of the Nile were measured by devices that have come to be known as Nilometers. These were of three types: The earliest and simplest Nilometer

Observers monitor the height of the Nile by measuring the water's rise and fall on an obelisk known as a Nilometer, built in a well that is connected to the river. Located on the island of Roda at Cairo, the Nilometer shown in this 19th Century engraving dates back to 715 A.D.

Egyptian villagers gather beside a flooded valley near the Giza pyramids southwest of Cairo in this 1900 photograph. Before the construction of dams along the Nile, such basins were naturally irrigated each year by floodwaters that saturated the land from August until October, when planting began.

involved only readings from marks engraved on rocky banks of the river; almost as simple were readings taken from flights of steps that edged into the waters; the third method was the most accurate, and utilized tunnels to carry water from the Nile to a cistern or well. As the level of the water rose inside the well it was measured and recorded either on the outer walls of the well or on a fixed central column.

Such a Nilometer was in use on Roda Island at Cairo. And in ancient times, when the mark at Roda showed 16 cubits (one cubit equals approximately 18 inches, based on the distance between the elbow and the tip of the middle finger), it was a sign for the dikes to be opened so that the floodwaters could move into the adjoining lowland enclosures through a series of small canals controlled by gates.

There, saturating the land with their nutrient-rich sediment, the floodwaters were allowed to stand at a depth of up to six feet for six to eight weeks. Then, after the flood had receded, the gates were again opened and the life-giving water drained back into the river.

When the system worked, Egypt was an object of envy. Great crops of barley, wheat and millet were harvested. This was the *wafa,* or time of bounty, and festivals were held honoring Hapi, the god of the Nile, and the goddess Isis, whose tears determined the stage of the river. The Egyptians, wrote Herodotus, "obtain the fruits of the field with less trouble than any other people in the world." But the bounty was limited: Egypt lacked water-storage facilities and, with the annual flood confined to the late-summer months, farmers could raise only one crop a year.

In some doleful years there were practically no crops at all, for the Nile was often notably unhelpful. At times the flood failed to rise to sufficient levels and, with the soil deprived of its yearly wetting, famine followed. "For seven years," lamented one Pharaoh, "the Nile has not risen. There is no grain, the fields are dry. Everyone flees, to return no more, the children weep, the young men faint, the old men wither."

As often as there was drought there was flooding. At such times the river rose far beyond the levels required to feed the land, breaching the natural levees along its banks or drowning the embankments that had been built to trap the water for irrigation. Sir William Willcocks, a British dam designer, described the pandemonium that accompanied a levee break in 1887: "The villagers rushed out on to the banks with their children, their cattle and everything they possessed. The confusion was indescribable. A narrow bank was covered with buffaloes, children, poultry and household furniture. The women assembled round the local saint's tomb, beating their breasts, kissing the tomb, and uttering loud cries, and every five minutes a gang of men running into the crowd and carrying off the first thing they could lay hands on wherewith to close the breach.

"The fellaheen meanwhile plunged into the breach, stood shoulder to shoulder across the escaping water, and with the aid of torn-off doors and windows and Indian corn stalks, closed the breach."

At one point Willcocks talked to a man of apparently advanced years who had been especially active in stemming the flood tide. "He told me that he was a comparatively young man," Willcocks recalled, "but he had had charge of the Nile bank when a great breach occurred in 1878, and that Ismail Pasha had telegraphed orders to throw him and the engineer into the breach. He was given twelve hours grace by the local chief, and during that interval his hair had become white." Subsequently, reported Willcocks, the man was pardoned, presumably because the breach was successfully stemmed.

During the 19th Century the Egyptians took steps to increase the amount of arable land and to lengthen the growing season. They built a network of canals leading to fields planted in cotton; the canals retained the water until it was needed in the dry summer months. And under British auspices early in the 20th Century, six flood-control dams, including the edifice now known as the Old Aswan Dam, were erected on the Nile. Although the reservoirs behind the dams stored sufficient water to permit some year-round irrigation, by the end of World War II their capacity was hopelessly inadequate to meet the nation's agricultural needs: Egypt's population had doubled between 1897 and 1946—and it was to double again during the next 30 years.

Moreover, the dams failed to stop the floods that from time to time ravaged entire villages. Even though the height of the Old Aswan Dam was raised twice, the structure still could not hold the summer flooding and the mighty burden of silt. During flood, the dam's gates had to be left open to permit the silt-laden water to flow through, otherwise the reservoir behind the dam would have been overburdened with silt, shrinking its capacity and putting the dam at risk as well.

The High Dam at Aswan, then, was built to fulfill a people's most basic yearnings. And after the Nile was diverted and construction on the High Dam had begun, crowds gathered outside the Egyptian Parliament building in Cairo and chanted: "Nasser, Nasser, we come to salute you. After the dam our land will be paradise."

The High Dam at Aswan may have held out a promise of paradise to Egypt's people, but from its very inception it has provoked tempests of controversy among scientists of every sort, from hydrologists and archeologists to climatologists and agricultural economists. And the debates have not diminished in intensity since the dam went into operation.

Completed in 1970, the High Dam is a behemoth. "The great rockfill mass blocking the Nile is so large that it seems a part of the rocky relief of the region," wrote an American scientist who visited the site. "Hundreds of thousands of boulders well over two yards in diameter litter the faces of the dam like small pebbles, and the feathery spume ejected from the tailraces arching 90 feet or more into the air dwarfs the passing workers."

Designed by West German engineers and subsequently modified by the Soviets, the massive structure spans 11,812 feet between the granite wall of the east bank and the sand hills of the west; standing 364 feet high, it is an astounding 3,215 feet thick at its base, 131 feet at the crest—in bulk, 17 times larger than the Great Pyramid at Giza.

With a road and railway running along its massive span, the Old Aswan Dam, pictured in this turn-of-the-century photo, cleaves the Nile 590 miles above Cairo and four miles north of the future site of the High Dam at Aswan. Built in 1902 by the British, the old masonry dam towered 90 feet above the river, allowing the Egyptians for the first time to store water for irrigation during the dry season.

By any measure, Egypt's High Dam across the Nile at Aswan is a stupendous feat of civil engineering. When it was completed in 1970 after more than a decade of construction and the expenditure of one billion dollars, it stood as the greatest flood-control and hydroelectric project in all of Africa. Indeed, it ranked among the first half dozen such works throughout the world.

Undertaken as a joint venture by Egypt and the Soviet Union, which provided technical and financial help, the project was monumental in every respect. The engineers meant to capture the Nile at a point where it was one third of a mile across and 100 feet deep in its central channel. The dam itself was to withstand the pressure of a reservoir 300 miles long containing 1.25 million acre-feet of water. And a hydroelectric plant with a capacity of 2.1 million kilowatts was to supply much of Egypt's energy needs.

The final plan—based on an earlier design submitted by a West German firm—called for a colossal rockfill barrier encasing a central structure of sand, clay and concrete, and pegged to bedrock beneath the riverbed by a huge curtain of an epoxy-like grout. For added strength the design incorporated an arch that faced upstream and distributed the water pressure in a manner that helped lock the dam into the riverbanks.

Construction began in 1960 with the excavation of a diversion canal on the east bank. This canal, carved mostly out of granite, initially shunted the river around the construction site; later it became the dam's principal spillway and source of power.

Work also began on two rockfill cofferdams, one above and one below the site of the dam's core. The upstream cofferdam was designed to divert the river into the canal, the downstream dam to prevent erosion below the site and contain any fill materials escaping in the early stage of construction. At the same time, the sand base for the core was laid down, and compacted underwater in an innovative fashion (*overleaf*).

By 1964, more than 33,000 men were at work. The diversion canal was opened, the cofferdams were finished, and efforts focused on building the central dam itself. The work took six years, by which time millions of tons of rockfill had broadened the dam, engulfing both cofferdams to form a single gigantic barrier that contained a staggering 55 million cubic yards of material.

Stretching for more than two miles along its crest, the High Dam at Aswan, built in the decade of the 1960s, backs up an immense lake that covers 2,000 square miles of mostly desert land. At left is the great spillway and the hydroelectric plant. At right, a crownlike monument commemorates Egyptian and Soviet cooperation in the mammoth project.

Though built upon a bed of sand, the Aswan High Dam is as firmly founded as any dam in the world, due in no small part to its great curtain of grout and a Soviet-developed method of compacting sand to produce a stability approaching that of rockfill.

After a layer of fine dune sand 49 feet thick had been pumped in the form of slurry through pipes down onto the riverbed, special barge-mounted pylons were inserted into the material and were mechanically vibrated at 1,750 cycles per minute. This vibration greatly increased the density of the sand, compressing each layer by eight feet to a thickness of 41 feet. Two such layers were laid down to provide a hard, stable foundation for the dam.

The dam builders' method of rooting the structure to bedrock was no less ingenious. First they drilled a series of holes four inches in diameter—and as deep as 700 feet—down to bedrock below the river, and forced grout through perforated pipes into the surrounding sand. The grout from one hole spread until it linked with the grout from the next, about eight feet away. All told, 70 holes were grouted at different depths with mixtures of cement, clay and epoxy-like silicates to form a solid curtain 128 feet thick and 40 feet wide at its top.

Above the compacted sand and the grout curtain, a core of impermeable clay provided a spinelike mass elastic enough to absorb the inevitable settling movements in the foundation and any horizontal deformation due to lateral water pressure. Three inspection galleries were included in the clay core to allow access to the heart of the structure for monitoring seepage and deformation.

From the base of the dam a corrugated blanket of clay with an average thickness of 20 feet was extended 600 feet upstream to

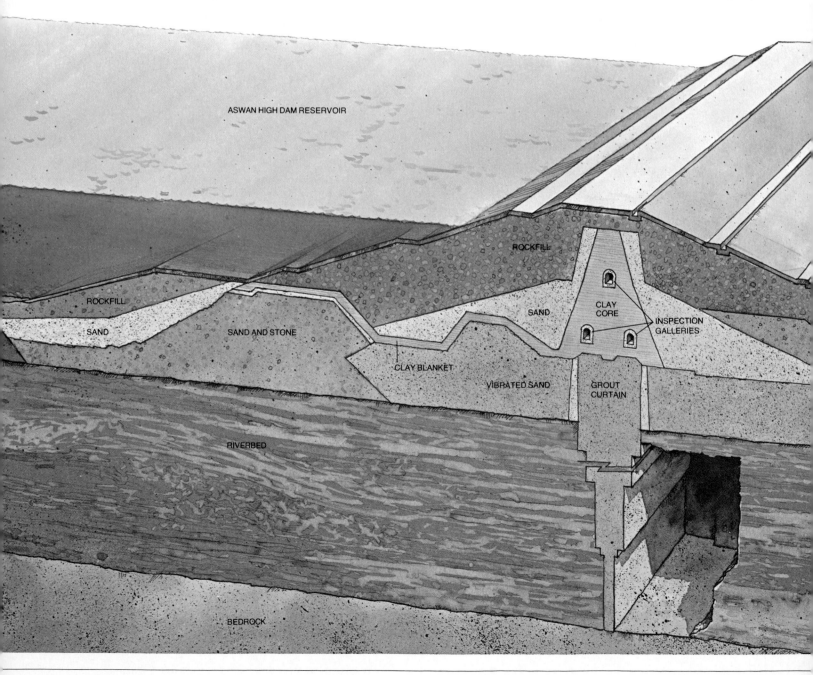

ASWAN HIGH DAM RESERVOIR

ROCKFILL

ROCKFILL

SAND

SAND AND STONE

CLAY BLANKET

SAND

CLAY CORE

INSPECTION GALLERIES

VIBRATED SAND

GROUT CURTAIN

RIVERBED

BEDROCK

the site of the cofferdam; its purpose was to prevent seepage from undermining the whole dam. The corrugated shape of the blanket provided a stronger bulwark against slippage on the upstream face than would a simple flat layer. On the dam's downstream side, drainage wells were drilled as a last line of defense against undermining by seepage.

Uppermost on the dam, layer upon layer of rockfill—29.6 million cubic yards—added tremendous mass to the structure. The rock also served to dissipate potentially damaging erosion by the wind-driven waves of the enormous reservoir.

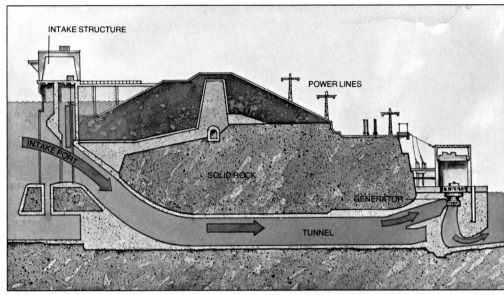

The Aswan High Dam's hydroelectric station is fed by six great tunnels like the one shown here in cross section. Water rushes into intake ports on the diversion canal and drops 255 feet inside a tunnel 49 feet in diameter, reaching the feeders for the hydroelectric generators at speeds as high as 85 mph. Each tunnel divides into two at the powerhouse, supplying 12 gigantic turbine generators, each capable of producing 175,000 kilowatts of electricity.

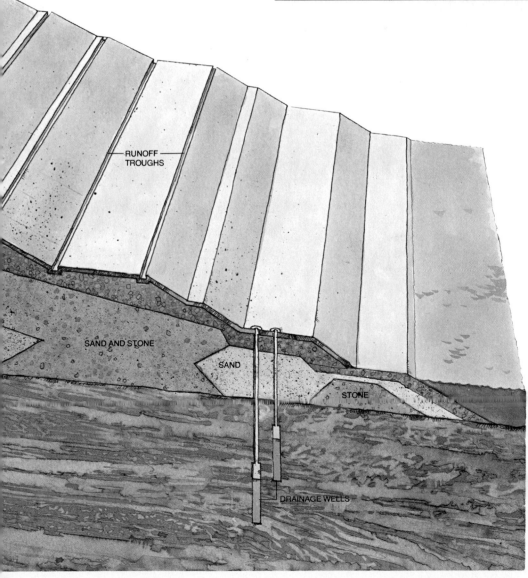

Yet the engineering genius of the dam lies less in its size than in the manner in which it is molded to the terrain, becoming almost a part of the earth. Because the river's bed at Aswan is mucky and unstable the dam has no solid rock foundation; instead, the great thickness of its base is intended to compensate by spreading the structure's weight over a very large area. The upstream face is so gradually sloped that sediments settle upon it in natural layers, and the dam presents no perpendicular front to receive the full thrust of the Nile's water.

Stretching southward behind the High Dam through 200 miles of Egyptian territory and another 100 of Sudanese (from which 100,000 Nubians were evacuated, much against their will) lies the Aswan High Dam Reservoir. Of the lake's total capacity of 136 million acre-feet of water, the deepest 26 million is kept as dead storage—meaning that it is below the level of the dam's spillway and is set aside for the accumulation of silt. Despite gloomy forecasts by the dam's early critics that the reservoir would rapidly fill with sediment, later and more realistic estimates have given it a useful life of at least 300 years.

The next 73 million acre-feet of water is held in live storage, so that it can be released in controlled amounts and used for irrigation throughout the year. Space for another 37 million acre-feet is available to contain the water of exceptionally high floods.

In its magnificent mass and with its far-reaching reservoir, the High Dam is thus able, on the one hand, to hold back the waters of ruinous floods and, on the other, to serve the year-round needs of Egypt's agriculture and to provide energy for industry and homes. More than 725,000 acres have been added to the Egyptian farmland receiving perennial irrigation, bringing the total to 5.7 million acres, or 100 per cent of the nation's arable land. Two or three crops a year are now commonplace and rice production, for example, has quintupled.

Because irrigation has been given priority over hydroelectric requirements, the dam's annual power output of 7.5 billion kilowatt hours is short of its 10-billion capacity; nevertheless, the dam is the source of more than half of Egypt's electrical production.

The High Dam has therefore fulfilled the major purposes for which it was constructed. Yet in many of its side effects—some of them predicted and others entirely unexpected—the dam has stirred bitter recriminations, to the point that at least one Egyptian scientist has urged a return to the seasonal flood and basin irrigation. Listing the complaints in 1975, Great Britain's respected *Economist* blamed the High Dam for "causing the erosion of the Egyptian coastline, killing the sardine industry, depriving the delta of the yearly flood silt that gave Egypt the world's most fertile soil, and spawning a plague of the dangerous bilharzia parasite."

Placing such charges in better perspective were the 1980 findings of a team of 120 Egyptian and 25 American scientists, headed by Egypt-born Khalil Mancy, a professor of environmental chemistry at the University of Michigan, and jointly sponsored by the Ford Foundation and the United States Environmental Protection Agency. After five years of what was probably the most intensive study ever undertaken of a river and reservoir, Mancy's group concluded that "early prognostications of the damaging side-effects of the dam have been greatly exaggerated" and the High Dam "has been an unqualified economic success." While dam maintenance cost Egypt $844 million in the decade between 1970 and 1980, the benefits derived from it have been estimated at $1.1 billion.

Still, by depriving the valley of the Nile of an ecosystem based on seasonal flooding waters, the edifice of Aswan has undeniably had effects that speak to the basic understanding of floods as part of the natural order.

The Nile's gift to Egypt is dramatically evident in this mosaic of infrared satellite photographs taken in 1972. Lush vegetation, which registers red in this photo, appears only in the well-watered Nile delta and along the course of the river as it winds 950 miles from Sudan to the Mediterranean; Lake Karoon, an ancient irrigation project, can be seen on the west bank, and a smaller, modern reclamation project appears on the east bank near the Aswan High Dam.

Before the High Dam was built, the Nile carried seaward each year an average of 100 million tons of sediment, of which approximately 13 million tons was deposited on Egypt's fields before reaching the Mediterranean. The silt was volcanic in its origin and, although largely deficient in nitrogen, was rich in potassium and phosphates, with nutritional trace elements of iron, zinc and magnesium.

That priceless load is now captured by the High Dam's reservoir, and the water released by the dam is virtually clear of sediment. The effect was felt almost immediately, and in 1974 Egypt's Agriculture Minister Sayyid Marei voiced his concern: "I say in all candor, as loudly as possible, I am worried, extremely worried, because of the threat to the fertility of our soils."

Egypt's answer to the problem was a large increase in the use of chemical fertilizers. But chemical fertilizers are expensive; in 1970 alone replacement of lost nutrients cost an estimated $80 million. However, there was no alternative. Farming accounts for 30 per cent of Egypt's gross national product and 80 per cent of its export earnings. Something had to be done to protect the nation's agriculture.

As with almost everything connected with the High Dam, the loss of the Nile's sediment has resulted in trade-offs between the beneficial and the damaging. Egypt's chemical fertilizer industry, spurred by agricultural demand and using hydroelectric power provided by the dam, has greatly expanded, creating many job opportunities at the five chemical plants that have opened to meet the increased demands; one of these plants, at Aswan, employs more than 10,000 workers.

At the same time, the once-prosperous brickmaking industry has suffered. The Nile's sediment, composed of 30 per cent fine sand, 40 per cent silt and 30 per cent clay, was ideal for bricks. In the pre-Aswan era the operators of about 7,000 kilns along the Nile got the material free of cost from canal cleanings. With that source cut off, the brickmakers were forced to buy topsoil from farmers, paying as much as $1,600 to remove about one yard's depth from an acre. Since Egyptian farmers average only about $200 annually per acre, they were delighted to accommodate the brick industry. The brickmakers, however, could ill afford the expense, and in the years after the dam, brick production showed little or no increase despite the needs of Egypt's growing population. Worse, large areas of farmland, stripped of rich topsoil, were lost to agriculture.

The crop yields of Egyptian farmland have been further retarded by problems of salinity and waterlogging, both of which have been at least indirectly aggravated by the existence of the High Dam. One of the most abundant materials in nature, sodium is found in many rocks; since it is highly soluble, it is one of the first elements taken from decaying rocks by moving water. When combined with chlorine, sodium forms common salt, which in its dissolved form is carried by rivers to the world's oceans and seas.

In areas where the rate of evaporation is high—such as the Nile valley, subjected as it is to the blaze of the African sun—the salt becomes so concentrated that it is precipitated out of the water. When the Nile's annual floods were allowed to spread over the land for a few weeks and then to recede, the accumulated salt deposits were largely flushed out. Since the building of the High Dam at Aswan, however, both chemical fertilizers and effluent from Egypt's increasingly crowded cities have added to the salt content of the Nile's water. And under perennial irrigation, with water standing for prolonged periods of time, the salt settles and permeates the upper levels of the soil where crops find their nourishment. Although salt is vital to animal life, it can be fatal to crops.

In their understandable enthusiasm for perennial irrigation, for so many centuries the object of their dearest hopes, Egyptian farmers have lavishly wa-

tered their fields—and thereby cc
as waterlogging. It has been estii
post-Aswan agriculture represent
water table, and since the supply
never has an opportunity to desc
actually drowned.

The combined effects of wate
study, published in 1975, indicat
suffered from salinity to some de,
afflicted by waterlogging. A later
suggested that the situation was
Egyptian agriculture is prey to the
ed that crop production was 30 to
lands than on unafflicted farms in

The most practical remedy for
better drainage, which can be acl
drains and pumping stations. Bu
the extent of the problems, work t
of the requirements created by raj
tion. As late as 1975, out of a tota
in the delta and 700,000 in Upp
inefficient open field drains.

Egypt has been struggling to i
drainage—but the costs are high
of Irrigation estimates that impi
million annually, enough to build
years. At present rates, the year
extends to four million acres.

That may be too late for some (
sessions which, like the farmland
Even while the High Dam and re:
obvious that unless something w
many of the ancient monuments i
the same time, it was firmly beli
for downstream monuments, prot
them for ages past.

Under the general auspices of
and Cultural Organization, a br
save the principal upstream moi
Kalabsha, 40 miles south of the
to higher ground, as was the ent
lae near Aswan (pages 157-159)
temple of Amada, 77 feet long a
half miles and raised more tha
niously powered by hydraulic pu
transported stone by stone on ba
just below the dam.

Most important of all, the two
achievements of Ramses II and tl
existed 3,200 years before, wer
separate sandstone slabs, the lar,
were hoisted by cranes to a new a

In all, 19 monuments were r
reservoir, the antiquarians had a
foreseen was that the downstream
more subtle force than massive in

and five miles. But in the first half of the 20th Century, the building of the Old Aswan Dam and other barriers inhibited the transportation of sediment and reversed the ratio between siltation and erosion, causing the two outlets to retreat by about 100 feet a year.

Then came the High Dam—and the silt-bearing floods stopped entirely. The pace of coastal erosion inevitably quickened, and the damage was no longer limited to the Rosetta and Damietta peninsulas. Much of the Egyptian coastline is now being gnawed away. Farms, villages and seaside resorts such as Baltim and Ras el Barr stand on the edge of extinction. By the time the High Dam was 10 years old only a quarter of a mile of vulnerable shoreline protected Ras el Barr from the sea, and some villages had already been abandoned to the hungry waves.

Even more worrisome, the peril of breaching hung over the slender spits of sand that separate the delta's shallow, brackish lakes from the Mediterranean. Near the Rosetta outlet, for example, the sea had already encroached in one place on Lake Burullus. At most it lay less than 1,500 feet from the lake. As the sea breaks into the lakes, they become bays of the Mediterranean, and subterranean seepage of their more salty water could ruin as many as one million acres of cultivated land. To prevent that calamity, Egypt may have to take resolute measures. "Sooner or later," said the University of Michigan's Khalil Mancy, "Egypt, like Holland, will have to build dikes."

Similarly, the loss of vast amounts of sediment to the reservoir has upset the delicate balance between the scouring action of the water and the deposition of silt around downstream bridges and a number of low barriers used to help regulate the river for irrigation; since the High Dam went into operation the unrelieved scouring action of the water has exposed these structures to the dangers of undermining. Yet in almost every aspect of its existence, the High Dam offers compensations—and in the matter of sedimentation, Egypt's loss is apparently Sudan's gain. Aided by satellite analysis of deposition patterns in the reservoir, Mancy's team found that the southern, or Sudanese, end of the reservoir has so far received nearly all of the Nile silt —to such an extent that a sizable new delta is building. Within the foreseeable future, according to Mancy, "the Sudanese will have a nice piece of property coming to them."

Sudan and Egypt alike have benefited from another gift of the reservoir. The still water of the lake has produced bumper crops of the microscopic zooplankton (animal organisms) and phytoplankton (plant life) that are basic to the food chain of fish. The reservoir has become a fishery that is profitable far beyond early expectations, with the commercial catch soaring from 750 tons in 1966 to 28,000 in 1979. The reservoir offers 57 varieties of fish, with the delectable Nile perch, which grows to 150 pounds, leading the way.

Yet, again, what the High Dam has given the High Dam has taken away. Downstream from the dam, increased chemical runoff from fertilizers, insecticides and herbicides, along with subtle ecological changes in the sediment-free river, have reduced the species of fish from 47 to 17. Compounding the depletion of the riverine fishery is the virtual disappearance of Egypt's Mediterranean sardine industry, which once produced about 30,000 tons a year. Before the High Dam was built, the Nile's floods annually discharged into the sea a vast population of phytoplankton, attracting schools of hungry sardines. Fifteen years later, with that food supply no longer available, the catch had dwindled to between 1,000 and 2,000 tons. Wrote an American scientist in Egypt: "I searched the fish markets of the delta coast and found not a single sardine at a time of year when they were previously abundant."

Yet another problem occurred in 1974 while the reservoir was filling. At the lowest levels of the reservoir, thermal stratification set in and a stag-

For more than 2,600 years the monuments on the tiny island of Philae near Aswan withstood the seasonal flooding of the Nile, as well as a succession of man-made disasters in the form of violent political and religious upheavals. But in the 1970s, after the construction of the Aswan High Dam, the temples of Philae appeared doomed by rising waters—until a remarkable feat of archeological engineering effected their rescue.

Long known as the Pearl of Egypt, Philae was adorned with some of history's most elegant and graceful temples. The oldest, an altar dedicated to the sun-god Amun, dates back to the Seventh Century B.C. Over succeeding centuries greater and lesser Pharaohs left their marks in stone at Philae, including the durable line of the Ptolemies, heirs of Alexander the Great. After Rome conquered Egypt in 30 B.C., Emperors Augustus, Tiberius, Hadrian and Trajan all endowed the 16-acre island with monuments.

The most serious destruction at Philae

came in the Sixth Century when Coptic Christian zealots defaced some of the pagan imagery. But that was nothing compared with the threat that arose in the 20th Century. After the height of the first Aswan dam was increased by the British in 1933, the waters of its reservoir inundated the island for nine months each year. And when construction of the new High Dam was begun 27 years later, the waters seemed certain to engulf Philae forever.

In the nick of time, however, the United Nations launched a dramatic effort to rescue the temples and their treasures. With $27 million in U.N. funds, engineers in 1972 surrounded the island with a stout cofferdam, pumped the water out of the enclosure, and carefully marked and mapped every monument and building. Then, stone by stone, the temples of Philae were dismantled and moved to the nearby island of Agilkia, where it took eight years to reassemble them in their original form on high ground.

Sitting in the middle of a man-made lake near Aswan, the sacred island of Philae is temporarily protected from the rising waters of the Nile by two concentric steel walls reinforced by more than one million cubic yards of sandfill. In the distance, framed by the broad front wall of the temple of Isis and the columnar kiosk of Trajan, a three-mile pipeline carries sand slurry to the cofferdam from the far shore.

Hauling their burdens in baskets much as their
ancestors did, laborers remove tons of mud—left by
decades of seasonal flooding—from the West
Colonnade at the temple of Isis. One hundred yards
long, the colonnade adorned the island's principal
quay with 32 tall columns, each topped with
a sculpted flower capital. The high-water mark is
clearly evident on the masonry and the columns.

Brushing a latex-rubber compound into the carvings
on a column, a worker at Philae prepares to
take an impression of the ancient sculpture and
hieroglyphs. Several layers of the compound
were applied, and when they had set, the coating was
peeled off the stonework bearing an exact impression
of the grooves. Such work was invaluable in realigning
stones during the reconstruction of the temples,
and it also assured that their priceless historical record
would be preserved in case of accident.

Carefully arrayed according to type and position, pieces of the ancient temples lie in a storage area before their reconstruction on the nearby island of Agilkia. All told, 45,000 stones, including one that weighed 18 tons, were removed and transported by barge to their new site, 43 feet higher than Philae.

Marked with white lines to facilitate reassembly, two sections of columns from Philae stand ready for transport to Agilkia, visible in the distance. Hieroglyphics within the oval cartouche on the stone at left identify a Ptolemaic king and proclaim, "May he live forever." Next to the scarab—an Egyptian symbol of resurrection—on the column at right, a defaced carving bears evidence of the vandalism inflicted by Coptic Christians in the Sixth Century.

nant layer developed. Within that unseen world, a multitude of microorganisms lived and died, and the biological decay of their residue, in a process known as eutrophication, consumed oxygen dissolved in the water, leaving anaerobic organisms—life that requires no oxygen—as the dominant presence. This in turn set off a chemical chain reaction that produced a blue-green algal slime that passed through the dam sluiceways and into the downstream Nile, contaminating urban water supplies. When combined with chlorine, the algae turned drinking water dark and gave off a highly offensive odor. Dam engineers have since taken care to flush the lowest levels of the reservoir by means of sluices in the base of the dam, thus preventing the recurrence of a stagnant layer.

The quality of the Nile's water has also been impaired by human and industrial wastes from the burgeoning cities. "Before the Aswan High Dam," Mancy reported, "the river cleansed itself annually. The Nile flood used to flush the accumulated waste into the sea. With increased river use after the dam, due to population increase and industrial activity, the impacts of waste discharges on river conditions are more pronounced."

As vile as the Nile's drinking water may sometimes appear, it has so far represented no great hazard to human health. The same cannot be said of the water that now stands year-round in Egypt's irrigation canals and ditches. Sluggish in its movement and rank with weeds, it is a perfect habitat for the Bulinus snail—which is, in turn, the innocent intermediate host to a parasite that has debilitated much of Egypt's peasantry.

Eggs of the Schistosoma worm float in the water until they hatch in the form of swimming larvae, which, to survive, must find a temporary home in the body of a Bulinus snail. There the larvae develop into fork-tailed microscopic worms, which, once their metamorphosis is complete, reenter the water.

It requires only a few moments for these pestilent little cercariae to bore through skin and work their way into the human body, which also serves as a host to the parasite. After moving through the bloodstream, the worms grow to adulthood in the veins of the abdominal cavity, laying astronomical numbers of eggs that can clog such vital organs as the bladder, liver and intestines. Some of the eggs are discharged in human excreta, and the subsequent hatch requires only more snails to start the cycle over again. The process takes about 11 weeks.

The result is a chronic disease named schistosomiasis (also known as bil-

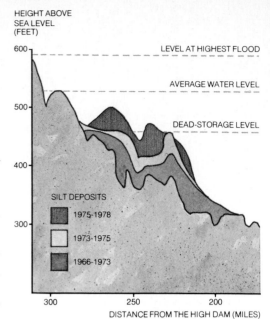

Nile silt, once carried downriver to enrich Egyptian cropland, now settles quickly in the southern half of the lake behind the High Dam, as shown in this cross section of the uppermost 125 miles of the reservoir. The amount of silt varies with seasonal floodwaters, but measurements indicate an overall rate of sedimentation higher than expected—rapid enough to fill much of the huge lake within 300 years.

In an irrigation canal near Sakkara, Egyptian children bathe and frolic while their mothers busy themselves with the day's washing. More than 54,000 miles of canals and irrigation ditches receive water on a year-round basis thanks to the High Dam.

harziasis) for which no effective cure has been found. Although fatal only in its complications, it manifests itself in numerous nasty ways, including blood in urine and stools, enlarged livers and spleens, hives, vertigo, epileptic seizures, and general lassitude and extreme irritability.

Schistosomiasis is a worldwide problem and it is no stranger to Egypt; the disease was known under the Pharaohs. However, before the 20th Century, with brief seasons of flood and irrigation, the country was far less hospitable to the Bulinus snail than modern Egypt is under the ecological regime of the dams and perennial irrigation. With water always available, Egyptian peasants constantly expose themselves to contact with the boring worms. Farmers slosh about in water while performing their daily chores. They use the infected water to conduct their ablutions before prayer. Many people bathe in the canals and ditches, and children play in the water. Moreover, the best educational efforts of health authorities have failed to break peasants of their habit of voiding into the water—thereby continuing the vicious parasitic cycle.

In their building of the High Dam at Aswan, the Egyptians reached for a piece of paradise. They received, and in many ways have been greatly benefited by, a flood-free habitat—but they also suffered in unexpected ways. In this paradox lies the essence of man's relationship to the planet upon which he exists.

Floods are as much a part of the natural order as rainbows or rain clouds. Throughout the world, people have chosen to live on the lands made fertile by floods—and these deluges, in their relentless turn, have exacted a high price. Even in those rare instances where human ingenuity has managed to hold the forces of flooding in thrall, the resulting imbalance of nature's equilibrium has imposed penalties that are often unforeseen and sometimes unforeseeable.

So it has always been. So, for as long as water falls upon the land, it will always be. In 1981, even as the Chinese in their millions continued the age-old struggle to protect the Great Plain of the Yellow from the river's ravages, the Yangtze, less than 700 miles to the south, broke out of its banks and drowned an estimated 3,000 humans. In the American Southwest, flash floods defied the best efforts of forecasters and, in Texas, killed 28 people. Throughout the vast expanse of the Mississippi's system, engineers continued to erect ramparts against that calamitous season when all or most of the river's main tributaries come to spate at the same time.

As for Egypt, it lies in the shadow of its dam—which, if it were to burst, would bring destruction to much of the nation's farmland and industry. In that catastrophic event, individual humans striving to escape the flood might well believe that a deluge had inundated the entire earth. Ω

Every June when the monsoons break, a three-month-long rainy season begins in the vast Ganges flood plain that stretches across northern India through the teeming agricultural states of Uttar Pradesh and Bihar. But the torrential rains do not generate the same sort of terrifying floods that devastate densely populated flood plains elsewhere in Asia. And the 200 million people who live along the Ganges have learned to accommodate their lives to the annual inundation.

Unlike the flat basins of the Yellow and Mississippi Rivers, the Ganges basin is trough-shaped, with mountains on either side. The river flows along the deepest track in the middle of a depressed valley some 10 to 50 miles wide. Thus, even in full spate, when the discharge of the Ganges exceeds 7.4 million gallons per second, its course remains relatively stable. While the Ganges may overtop its banks and spread as much as 20 miles onto its flood plain, it does so gradually, in restricted, predictable belts.

To be sure, there is damage and some death, but Indians generally take the floods in stride. The Ganga Flood Control Commission has improved drainage and built dams to lessen the impact of floods; when they arrive business continues more or less as usual. In the countryside, huts are built with raised floors and streets are cut deep and narrow to channel the floodwaters and speed their runoff. Each village has numerous high platforms for storing goods in flood emergencies. Basic staples, such as wheat, barley and gram, are sown in November and harvested before the rains. Then, water-resistant crops, such as rice and sugar cane, are planted so that they can be harvested after the flooding is over.

For untold centuries, the river has been "Mother Ganges"—the embodiment of the goddess Ganga and an essential adjunct to the spiritual life of Hindu India. Even during the rainy season, there is no letup in the pilgrims flocking to its waters. For to bathe in the Ganges is to wash away sin and to drink it is to earn merit. To die beside it, to be cremated on its banks and to have one's ashes cast upon its holy waters—that is the most fervent dream of every Hindu.

Citizens of Benares, one of India's oldest cities, stroll nonchalantly on a street awash in muddy waters and blocked by downed trees and utility poles during the annual monsoon flood in 1967. The rain-swollen Ganges can be seen in the background.

Resting from their labors, farm workers, their saris soaked by a downpour, huddle on an embankment overlooking the inundated fields. For all their flood problems, Indians welcome the cooling rains as relief from the scorching dry heat of April and May.

Farmers salvage soggy handfuls of maize from a submerged field in Monghyr in the state of Bihar. Even as the monsoon floods wash away the topsoil from some fields, they replenish it in others by leaving behind fresh deposits of clay, loam and silt.

Ankle-deep in Ganges water, an itinerant Benares barber shaves a customer; his equipment hangs from the railing where he has set up shop. During this 1967 flood, power failures caused some shops and offices to close, but sidewalk entrepreneurs and street vendors managed to ply their trades as always.

Undeterred by waist-high water, a rickshaw driver pedals two members of a Hindu priestly caste through Benares streets turned into an inland sea by the Ganges' summer overflow. In the background, an enterprising boatman hires out his gondola.

Engrossed in their game and oblivious of the floodwaters around them, two friends play chess on a raised wood platform in a Benares side street.

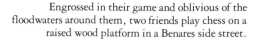

Their umbrellas forming a roof against the monsoon rain, a boatload of Benares-bound pilgrims cross the Ganges near the village of Sultanganj. Among the holiest of Indian cities, Benares is regarded by Hindus as the earthly capital of the god Siva, and plays host to some one million pilgrims every year.

Two *pandas,* Hindu priests who make their living selling religious accessories to pilgrims and guarding their belongings while they bathe, wait for the flooded Ganges to subside. Both men wear the sacred thread over their shoulders, indicating that they are twice-born in Hinduism's endless wheel of life.

Blissfully unconcerned about the rising waters, a man enjoys his afternoon nap on a makeshift raft in front of a padlocked storefront in Benares.

graphic Society. 105: Art by Richard Schlecht. 106, 107: Fil Hunter, except top right, art by Richard Schlecht. 108: National Oceanic & Atmospheric Administration, Environmental Research Labs. 110: Joel Radtke. 111: Professor Michael Charney. 112: National Environmental Satellite Service/National Oceanic & Atmospheric Administration. 114, 115: John P. Callahan for the *Providence Journal-Bulletin*. 116: Wide World. 117-119: Herbert Grube. 120, 121: Herbert Grube; Lewis L. Brown, courtesy The American Red Cross. 122, 123: Lewis L. Brown, courtesy The American Red Cross. 124: Pierre

Boulat/Cosmos, Paris. 127: Art by Richard Schlecht. 128: Courtesy California Historical Society/Title Insurance and Trust Company (Los Angeles) Collection of Historical Photographs. 129: Art by Richard Schlecht. 130, 131: Delmar Watson Hollywood Historical Archives. 133: Dale Howard/*Time*. 34: Art by Richard Schlecht. 135: Peter B. Kaplan. 137: Pierre Boulat/Cosmos, Paris. 140: Kurz & Allison, 1890, courtesy The New York Public Library, Print Room. 142: Courtesy Carnegie Library of Pittsburgh. 143: Johnstown Flood Museum. 144: Ralph Crane for *Life*. 146: Mary Evans Picture Library, London. 147, 148:

Library of Congress. 149: Fred Ihrt/Stern from Black Star © 1981. 150, 151: Art by Richard Schlecht. 152: The Nile River Project, The University of Michigan and the Egyptian Academy of Scientific Research and Technology. 154: Art by Richard Schlecht. 157: Dmitri Kessel, Paris. 158: Dmitri Kessel, Paris—UNESCO/Alexis N. Vorontzoff, Paris. 159: Soc. Italiana per Condotte d'Acqua, Rome—Dmitri Kessel, Paris. 160: Art by Richard Schlecht—Walter Weiss "Ägypten," C. J. Bucher, GmbH, Luzern, Switzerland, 1978. 162-171: © Raghubir Singh, Paris.

INDEX